D1077819

oM

LEABHARLANNA CHONTAE NA GAILLIMHE
(GALWAY COUNTY LIBRARIES)

Acc. No. M 110919   Class No. 920 CRO

Date of Return	Date of Return	Date of Return

Books are on loan for 21 days from date of issue.

Fines for overdue books: 10p for each week or portion of a week plus cost of postage incurred in recovery.

Oliver Cromwell

An Illustrated History

Helen Litton

Picture research by Peter Costello

WOLFHOUND PRESS
Celebrating 25 *Years*

First published 2000 by
WOLFHOUND PRESS Ltd
68 Mountjoy Square
Dublin 1

British Library Cataloguing in Publication Data
A catalogue record for this book is available from the British Library.

Extract from *The Tailor and Ansty* (page 7) reproduced by kind permission of
Mercier Press, Cork and Dublin, 1999.

'According to *The Moderate Intelligencer*' (page 44), from *Cromwell* by Brendan
Kennelly courtesy of Bloodaxe Books, 1987.

Illustration of Oliver Cromwell on page 91 courtesy of The National Gallery of
Ireland. Other copyright illustrations credited in captions.

The publishers have made every reasonable effort to contact the copyright holders
of material reproduced in this book. If any involuntary infringement of copyright
has occurred, sincere apologies are offered and the owners of such copyright are
requested to contact the publishers.

ISBN 0-86327-745-4

10 9 8 7 6 5 4 3 2 1

110919

£7.99

Cover design: Slick Fish Design, Dublin
Cover illustrations: Portrait of Oliver Cromwell, after Samuel Cooper
    (1609–1672) courtesy of the National Gallery of Ireland/The Siege of
    Drogheda, 1649 (contemporary engraving)
Typesetting and book design: Wolfhound Press
Printed in the Republic of Ireland by Techman, Dublin.

Contents

In memory of
Sister Mary Bertranda Flynn, OP.
Educator
18.5.1913–15.3.2000

Introduction

'Many years ago there was a man came to this country to do it a great harm. He was a man by the name of Cromwell. A sour-faced divil if ever there was one. He would shoot anyone he saw smiling. Before he came Ireland was known the world over as a country of laughter and fun and sport of every kind. Cromwell came with his army to stop all that. That was a long time ago. But it looks now to me that he left a lot of descendants....'

(*THE TAILOR AND ANSTY*)

That is one take on the legend of Oliver Cromwell in Ireland – the puritan kill-joy who destroyed harmony and peace. Many legends hang around his name, in both England and Ireland – 'church-destroyer', although he was responsible for very little of such destruction, 'religious bigot', although he believed (up to a point) in freedom of conscience, 'banisher of music and pleasure', although he enjoyed music in his home, and celebrated his daughters' weddings with much festivity. And there is also the reality of the affectionate family man, the regicide or king-murderer, the ruthless military commander who did not flinch from massacre, the Lord Protector who refused the title of king but ruled with almost regal ostentation.

What is one to make of such a deeply complex character? In Ireland, there has never been any doubt. Cromwell is remembered for one thing only – a brief but vicious military campaign whose blood soaks the pages of Irish history still, in both legend and reality. The shocked and demoralised country he left behind as he sailed back to England created a monster, to encapsulate the effect he had had: a bogeyman, used not just to scare children but to justify bloody insurrection. His campaign is seen as an indictment of English policy in Ireland, an extreme manifestation of the contempt and bigotry that underlay much English reaction to Ireland and the Irish.

The year 1999 marked the four hundredth anniversary of the birth of Oliver Cromwell. As England commemorated the man who saved it from royal absolutism and helped to consolidate parliamentary government, how did Ireland remember him?

This book deals with an extremely complex period in the interlinked history of Ireland, England, Scotland and Wales, and the bibliography gives some idea of the amount of material available, and the extent of recent research.

I want to thank Peter Costello for his usual meticulous picture research, and Wolfhound Press for publishing this volume, which is the fifth in the series of Illustrated Histories.

Oliver Cromwell

1: Cromwell the Man

Motto:

'Pax Quaeritur in Bello'

(Peace is Sought in War)

Early Life

Oliver Cromwell was born on 25 April 1599, at Huntingdon in Bedfordshire, England. He was the only son of seven surviving children of Elizabeth Steward and Robert Cromwell, who was the second son of a knight. Robert Cromwell's surname should have been Williams; his Welsh father had changed it on marrying the sister of Thomas Cromwell, one of King Henry VIII's most powerful councillors.

Oliver went to school in Huntingdon, and in 1616 spent some time at Cambridge University, but he was never known as a scholar. In 1617 his father died, and he returned home to support his mother and sisters. He had an extremely close and loving relationship with his mother who supported him all his life until her death at the age of 89.

In 1620 he married Elizabeth Bourchier and their first child, Robert, was born the following year. It was a successful marriage; thirty years later, Oliver was still writing 'to my dear, who is very much in my heart'. Robert was followed by Oliver junior, Bridget, Richard, Henry and Elizabeth (born 1629, his favourite child), and later by Mary and Frances (born 1637 and 1638). Oliver's early adult life followed that of any country squire of the time, absorbed in his family and property. He took some interest in local politics, but it was not until the age of 41 that he moved on to a wider stage.

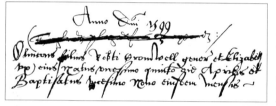

Cromwell's baptismal certificate from Huntingdon Parish Church, above which a later Royalist hand added, 'England's plague for five years'

Politics in England

In 1625 Charles I, aged 24, came to the throne of England, succeeding his father, the Stuart James I. Charles had unexpectedly become heir to the throne when his older brother, Henry, died tragically in 1616. He overcame childhood health problems to become a skilled horseman and swordsman, as well as a scholar and a student of theology. After becoming king, he married Henrietta Maria, a French Catholic princess. During his early reign, he followed the advice of the feckless Duke of Buckingham, but after Buckingham's death he was increasingly influenced by his queen.

Charles strongly supported the established Church of England in public, but many Protestants suspected him of Catholic leanings because of his marriage. Memories of Queen Mary I (Bloody Mary) and her attempts to overturn the Reformation were still powerful in England. At this period in time, the Church of England was being challenged by Puritanism, a strongly personal

Protestantism which believed that a structured church did nothing but come between God and man, with unnecessary complication; man's relationship with God should be personal, based on the Bible. The more extreme Puritans refused to accept the validity of any other forms of Protestantism, and all Puritans abhorred Catholicism. Religion was therefore a factor alienating the king from his parliament.

Normally, parliament met only when the king summoned it, and could be left dormant for many years. However, if the king needed exceptional sums of money, parliament had to be called so that a vote could be taken. Members of parliament were worried about the 'royal prerogative', that is, the king's power to levy some taxes without parliamentary permission whenever he thought fit. In 1628, they presented Charles with a Petition of Right, a list of complaints about, for example, arrest without trial, and arbitrary taxation. Although he accepted the petition, Charles stated firmly that he had to account for his actions only to God. However, England was at war with both France and Spain, and eventually, because the treasury needed large amounts of money urgently, he had to summon parliament in 1628, however little he wished to.

Cromwell in Public Life

Oliver Cromwell attended this, his first parliament, as an elected burgess for Huntingdon. Many of his extended family were politicians; nine of his cousins sat in the same parliament with him. He joined the parliamentary Committee on Religion, which was inquiring into 'popery' in England. The members of this parliament refused to adjourn themselves until a motion condemning popery and illegal subsidies was passed, and the Speaker was forcibly held down by some members until this was done. Parliament was not called again for eleven years.

Shortly after this, Cromwell seems to have gone through a period of depression or spiritual malaise of some kind, from

The skyline of Westminster in 1647, after a plan by Wenceslas Hollar, showing parliament (left), Westminster Hall (centre), where the king was tried, and the Abbey

which he emerged with a renewed faith, and a confidence in his personal relationship with God. Throughout his life he experienced these occasional withdrawals, and also suffered from a form of periodic malaria. He has been described as 'manic depressive', because of his frenzied outbursts of activity and passion. He could lose his temper furiously on occasion, but was generally friendly in manner and willing to listen to argument.

He may have considered taking ship for America, the New World, as many Puritans had done when they despaired of seeing change in England, but in 1636 he received an inheritance from his uncle, Sir Thomas Steward, which gave him an income of £400–£500 per annum, making him financially secure for the first time. He and his family moved to Ely, in the Fen Country.

Gathering Clouds

Charles I had appointed Dr William Laud as Archbishop of Canterbury. Laud supported the Arminians – Protestants who had a leaning towards ceremony and ritual and were in favour of a church hierarchy. They believed salvation was available to all, whereas the more Calvinist Puritans believed in the predestination of souls. Charles, with the help of Laud, wanted to impose religious orthodoxy over the whole of the British Isles, but the Puritans were determined to resist this.

The king was also overstretching his use of the royal prerogative. 'Ship-money', an occasional tax for defence spending, was now becoming a permanent tax, and was to be collected over the whole country, not just in coastal towns as before. A cousin of Cromwell's, John Hampden, refused to pay, and was sent to prison. Three Puritans who published material critical of the king had their ears cut off in punishment, and resentment of the king's behaviour began to spread.

In 1638, a religious revolt took place in Scotland. Charles had laid down a new liturgy and Prayer Book, and it had been rejected by Scottish religious leaders who resisted the authority of the Church of England. Instead, they published a 'National Covenant' which aimed to establish Presbyterianism, a form of Protestantism without bishops or any other formal hierarchical structure. They declared their loyalty to the king, but not to his religious innovations, and claimed to defend the true religion. Charles tried to enforce his wishes in the 'First Bishops' War', which ended without a battle. A treaty was signed at Berwick in 1639, but the Scottish Presbyterian General Assembly still condemned the idea of bishops and continued to resist control by the king. The treaty was obviously nothing more than a temporary ceasefire.

A coffee house in the 1600s (an innovation at that time) in which the politics of the day were keenly debated

Archbishop Laud

The English parliament was summoned again in 1640 (the 'Short Parliament') and this time Cromwell, aged 41, attended as elected burgess for Cambridge. He was mourning the death of his eldest son, Robert, who had died at school, aged 17 ('which went as a dagger to my heart'). A contemporary describes Oliver as being plainly dressed, grubby and untidy, his face 'swollen and reddish' and his voice 'sharp and untunable', but his eloquence was noticed by many, although he was still almost unknown in the House of Commons.

The Short Parliament, annoyed at the long gap since parliament had last been called, was hostile to Charles and wanted its grievances listened to before it would vote any money. It was soon dissolved, but before the members dispersed, John Pym, one of the oldest members, appealed for parliament to sit annually. The king would not listen. He embarked on the 'Second Bishops' War', which he lost in one battle in August 1640. He then had to call parliament together again, as his finances were drained. This became the 'Long Parliament'. It was to last for thirteen years, and during its life the political landscape of England would be transformed.

Cromwell, who was a deeply committed Christian, became a leading member of the Independent group in parliament. The Independents held that religious authority should rest only with local communities, who could decide their own path, outside the authority and preaching of the Church of England. The other main influence in parliament at the time was the Presbyterian group. Scotland wanted to move closer to union with England, but was insisting on the condition that Presbyterianism should be made the state church.

In 1641, the English commons passed the Protestation, which confirmed the 'true religion' (Protestantism). Meanwhile, Puritan movements were spreading, such as Sabbatarianism (keeping Sunday free from entertainments) and the removal of pictures and statues ('graven images') from churches.

Moves to Civil War

From Ireland's point of view, the most important event of 1641 was the rising against Protestant settlers (see Chapter 2) which confirmed the English view that Irish Catholics were vicious, bloody and ruthless, and could not be trusted. Exaggerated tales of cold-blooded murder and brutal massacres were fully believed, especially the role of Catholic priests in the murder of innocent Protestants. The parliamentary Committee for Irish Affairs set up fourteen commissioners, one of whom was Cromwell, to organise the raising of troops to pacify Ireland. Scotland was persuaded to send General Robert Munro with 10,000 men to Ulster, where order was restored and Presbyterianism established. Cromwell was among many who paid £2,000 for a grant of Irish land as an investment; his grant seems to have been in County Offaly.

The relationship between king and commons continued to deteriorate. Parliament had been shocked by the Bishops' Wars, which showed the lengths to which Charles would go in order to get his own way. A Triennial Act was passed, ruling that there were to be no more than three years between parliaments, and that parliament could not be dissolved without its own consent – thus cutting across the king's right of dissolution. Subsequently, Charles visited Scotland, giving rise to suspicions that he was seeking to make peace with the Scots and enlist their help against his own parliament.

Parliament produced a powerful attack on the position of the monarchy, called the Grand Remonstrance. This proposed drastic changes, but was not intended to overturn the whole political system. The commons simply disliked and distrusted Charles himself, and wished to reduce his powers. Charles, supported by the House of Lords, tried to arrest some of the leaders of this movement in January 1642, but they escaped. He left London to gather his forces, while the queen headed for the continent to sell her jewels. Parliament began to raise troops on its own behalf. There had been no real state army since the time of Henry VIII, but there was a nominal militia of 'trained bands', about 160,000 men in all, which parliament could use as the nucleus of an army. Charles would have to raise and finance his own troops.

Parliament presented 'Nineteen Propositions' to the king, but they were rejected, and events progressed inexorably. As the MP Ralph Verney said, 'Peace and our liberties are the only thing we aim at; till we have peace I am sure we can enjoy no liberties, and without our liberties I shall not heartily desire peace'. No-one was quite sure where all of this was leading. Many royalists were not happy with all of Charles' actions, but felt it was better to support the monarchy and hope to reform it, rather than risk chaos.

First Civil War

Cromwell's first military activity was, as MP for Cambridge, to seize a convoy of treasure worth £20,000 which was heading from the university towards the king, and to claim it for parliament. This was a dangerous action, for war had not officially begun and he could have been accused of stealing it for himself, rather than requisitioning it for parliament. He was demonstrating his ability to make quick decisions, and to mobilise troops efficiently. He had already paid for the raising of two troops of volunteers. Parliament later protected him against charges of theft.

On 22 August 1642, Charles I raised his flag at Nottingham, and war had officially begun. For our purposes, there is little need to explore all the phases of the English Civil Wars. The most important aspect for us is the gradual transformation of Oliver Cromwell from a minor county squire to one of the greatest

military leaders England has known. His major achievement was
the establishment of a professional army, the New Model Army,
known as 'Ironsides' (or derisively as 'New Noddle Army' or
'Roundheads'), which ultimately defeated the royal forces.

Taking arms for the first time at the age of 43, Oliver
Cromwell refined and developed the cavalry charge, the most
important element of a battle. He saw attack as the best form of
defence; to him, war was a bloody, dirty business, to be got
through as quickly and efficiently as possible. He encouraged his
troops to charge as a united body, but he was also able to control
them after the charge, so that they regrouped instead of chasing
wildly after the enemy. He wanted religious men as his soldiers
and instituted a strict discipline, because he believed that God
would only support Godly men. He was popular with the troops,
and inspired loyalty. By January 1644 he was a Lieutenant-
General, and the battle of Marston Moor in July of that year saw
the first real setback for Charles' army – 'God made them as stub-
ble to our swords,' Oliver wrote afterwards.

*John Hampden makes his protest against the 'ship-money', a key event in the
years leading up to the Civil Wars. (Drawing by Ellis Silas)*

Parliament, worried by the slow pace of the war and several defeats by royalist forces, passed the Self-Denying Ordinance. This prevented members of parliament from acting as army officers, because too many of them were inexperienced, and professional commanders were obviously needed. Cromwell seems to have been ready to lay down his own command if this move would help in the development of a fully professional army. However, parliament found that it could not do without him, and the Self-Denying Ordinance was quietly forgotten in his particular case.

The battle of Naseby, in June 1645, was Oliver's first as senior commander, and it saw the final defeat of the king's troops. 'When I saw the enemy draw up and march in gallant order towards us ... I could not (riding about my business) but smile out to God in praises, in assurance of victory ... and God did it,' he wrote afterwards. 'O that men would therefore praise the Lord, and declare the wonders that He doth for the children of men!' Papers captured from the king's baggage revealed that he had been planning to recruit Irish Catholic troops, promising them religious concessions. The Scots offered peace to Charles I, and in April 1646 he fled to the shelter of their army, at Newark. Oxford, his headquarters, surrendered. The first civil war was over.

> *...For what do the enemy say? Nay, what do many say that were friends at the beginning of the Parliament? Even this — that the Members of both Houses have great places and commands, and the sword into their hands; and, what by interest in the Parliament, what by power in the Army, will perpetually continue themselves in grandeur, and not permit the War speedily to end, lest their own power should determine with it. This that I speak here to our own faces is but what others do utter abroad behind our backs. I am far from reflecting on any. I know the worth of those commanders, members of both houses, who are yet in power. But, if I may speak my conscience without reflection upon any, I do conceive if the Army be not put into another method, and the War more vigorously prosecuted, the people can bear the War no longer, and will enforce you to a dishonourable peace....*
>
> Speech by Cromwell in parliament, 9 December 1644
> (before the Self-Denying Ordinance)

Cromwell's Account of the Battle of Naseby

For the Hon William Lenthall, speaker of the Commons House of Parliament: these

Sir,

Being commanded by you to this service, I think myself bound to acquaint you with the good hand of God towards you and us.

We marched yesterday after the King, who went before us from Daventry to Harborough; and quartered about six miles from him. This day we marched towards him. He drew out to meet us; both armies engaged. We, after three hours fight very doubtful, at last routed his army; killed and took about 5,000, very many officers, but of what quality we yet know not. We took also about 200 carriages, all he had; and all his guns, being 12 in number, whereof two were demi-cannon, two demiculverins, and (I think) the rest sackers. We pursued the enemy from three miles short of Harborough to nine beyond, even to sight of Leicester, whither the King fled.

Sir, this is none other but the hand of God; and to Him alone belongs the glory, wherein none are to share with Him.... I wish this action may beget thankfulness and humility in all that are concerned in it. He that ventures his life for the liberty of his country, I wish he trust God for the liberty of his conscience, and you for the liberty he fights for. In this he rests, who is

Your most humble servant,
OLIVER CROMWELL
Haverbrowe,
14 June 1645

Since Cromwell was now in a position of some authority, his family moved to London. (His favourite daughter, Elizabeth, had just married John Claypole, and shortly afterwards Bridget Cromwell married Henry Ireton.) He was voted lands worth about £6,000 a year in thanks for his wartime achievements. However, in parliament he had less influence because the Presbyterians were in a majority over the Independents. Both English and Scottish

110,919
)

Presbyterians wanted to preserve the constitutional monarchy in order to establish a state church, but Independents such as Cromwell, who opposed the idea of a state church, were moving towards the abolition of the monarchy, or at least a reduction of its powers.

At Newark, Charles was blowing hot and cold over committing himself to the Scottish Solemn League and Covenant, and the Scots, tiring of his indecision, more or less offered to sell him to the English parliament. An agreement was signed in December 1646. He was handed over after a payment of £400,000, and placed in custody at Holdenby Hall, in Northamptonshire. Meanwhile, Oliver Cromwell had again been overcome by illness and depression, and kept out of public affairs for a while.

Parliament and the King

The army was now a considerable power in the political system, and parliament found it was having to listen to its troops and their complaints. They were owed over £300,000 in arrears of pay. Parliament wanted to disband them, offering them six weeks' worth of the months of pay they were owed. A new force would then be organised for service in Ireland, where the political situation was looking grave.

Cavaliers

Cromwell, overcoming his depression, involved himself in this stand-off, and tried to hold a middle way. He believed absolutely in proper authority and, to him, parliament was the elected authority which the army should therefore not oppose. However, he understood the army's legitimate grievances, and knew they should be responded to. Political extremists, who were called 'Levellers' because they wanted to 'level' all social classes, were active within the army. They wanted a wider franchise, leading to a property-owning democracy, with freedom of conscience. The king – a pawn in this game – was seized by the army Independents and moved to Cambridge, where he negotiated with them for his freedom. He was simultaneously and secretly negotiating with the Scots, offering to establish Presbyterianism in Scotland in exchange for their support.

The English population was mainly royalist, and the people were increasingly uneasy about seeing their king being pushed from pillar to post. The countryside had been ravaged by the civil war and the economy was in poor shape, with bad harvests. More religious rules were being laid down for public behaviour and this was resented. The army was also resented because it was so expensive, and calls were made for it to be disbanded. Parliament was in sympathy with this last demand, but when riots broke out in London, parliament had to call on the army to defend it.

Roundheads

Oliver Cromwell rides through York after its surrender.
(From a painting by Ernest Crofts)

Second Civil War

Charles, given confidence by disagreement among his enemies
and by his contacts with Scotland, suddenly disowned the 'Heads
of the Army Proposals' to which he had just agreed. Cromwell,
who had begun to think more kindly of the king, was disgusted

by this and resumed his old mistrust. Cromwell was gradually becoming a politician as well as a soldier. He did not want to see the end of the monarchy, simply the abdication of Charles I and the supremacy of parliament, but this position became increasingly difficult as Charles displayed more and more what was seen by parliament as duplicity. Charles, who was deeply committed to the doctrine of the 'Divine Right of Kings', did not seriously engage in talks with his inferiors. To him, a sovereign and a subject were two quite different things. He could not in conscience turn aside from his own convictions, no matter what it would cost him.

The king secretly signed an agreement with the Scots, promising to confirm Presbyterianism in England for three years. A royalist uprising took place in Wales, and Cromwell marched off to deal with it. This was the start of the second civil war. The Scots, although divided about the wisdom of invading England, crossed the border in support of Charles in July 1648, and there were royalist risings in Essex and Kent. Cromwell led his men north from Wales to meet the Scots, and at the battle of Preston defeated them completely; they lost 2,000 men, to his 100 losses. He agreed terms, and the second civil war ended. He was then astounded to learn that parliament was considering making further overtures to King Charles, seemingly prepared to trust him again.

It was obvious to Cromwell that this parliament would have to go.

Trial and Execution of the King

In November 1648, the army issued a 'Remonstrance', calling for democratic elections and the trial of the king on charges of treason to the parliament. They also thought about charging him with 'sacrilege', because he had ignored the direct verdict of God at the Battle of Naseby. Parliament postponed consideration of the Remonstrance, and the General Council of the army decided to move on London to put pressure on them. Parliament then rejected the Remonstrance, by 125 votes to 58. Cromwell had not taken part in this debate; he may have hoped parliament would reform itself without his public influence. By the time he arrived in London on 6 December, 'Pride's Purge' had taken place; Colonel Pride and other members of the army had driven most of the parliamentarians out by force, and only eighty were left. This was now the 'Rump Parliament'. Cromwell was opposed for a time to bringing the king to trial, but finally, on 26 December, he made a speech in which he rejected the king and his authority.

An act was passed to permit the trial of the king, and this began on 20 January. Charles refused to accept the right of parliament to try him. He would not recognise the court, or try to defend himself. He was sentenced to death, and executed on 30 January 1649, his death warrant signed by 59 MPs. Cromwell's name was third on the list. Cromwell was later accused of having wanted to be sole ruler himself, but this was not a likely outcome at the time. He seems simply to have become convinced that as long as Charles I lived, there would be no peace in England.

Act Abolishing the Office of King, March 1649

Whereas Charles Stuart, late King of England, Ireland, and the territories and dominions thereunto belonging, hath by authority derived from parliament been and is hereby declared to be justly condemned, adjudged to die, and put to death, for many treason, murders, and other heinous offences committed by him, by which judgement he stood, and is hereby declared to be attained of high treason, whereby his issue and posterity, and all others pretending title under him, are become incapable of the said crowns, or of being king or queen of the said kingdom or dominions, or either or any of them....

Be it therefore enacted and ordained ... that the office of a king in this nation shall not henceforth reside in or be exercised by any one single person; and that no one person whatsoever shall or may have, or hold the office, style, dignity, power, or authority of king of the said kingdoms and dominions, or any of them, or of the prince of Wales, any law, statue, usage, or custom to the contrary thereof in any wise notwithstanding....

Charles I (Courtesy of The National Gallery of Ireland)

This execution of a monarch was an earth-shattering event, which was met with revulsion in England, and reverberated throughout Europe. A king was almost sacred, the anointed of God, not just an ordinary man. A blow had been struck at the very foundations of monarchy. The trial judges, the 'regicides' as they were later called, were well aware that this was a momentous event. Cromwell himself was observed to be in a highly excited state, working himself up to this immense violation of the accepted order. It was believed by many that God would inflict some calamity to punish the country, but the regicides argued that it was lawful to kill a tyrant.

Charles did not seem to believe what was happening to him until sentence was passed. Although he is often seen as a weak, indecisive man, he died bravely, wearing two shirts for his public decapitation in case the January cold would make him shiver, and people would think he was shaking from fear. His goods were sold for the use of the Commonwealth, which was established in May. The House of Lords was abolished. Cromwell, while also preparing for his son Richard's marriage, began setting up his expedition to Ireland, which was becoming urgently necessary.

The execution of Charles I (from a contemporary woodcut)

2: The Situation in Ireland

Background

The first Anglo-Normans established themselves in Ireland in the twelfth century, and from that time English rulers had attempted to impose their rule on the whole island, with varying degrees of success. English government in Ireland was run from Dublin, and for many centuries was limited to Dublin and the counties around it, known as the Pale. Large areas of the country remained almost untouched by English authority, and England's constant fear was that some of her enemies, particularly the Catholic Spanish, could use Ireland as a 'back door' through which to invade.

In an effort to change this situation, the first properly planned and organised 'plantations' took place under the Tudors, particularly Elizabeth I, in the sixteenth century. Plantations worked on the principle that if you moved enough hard-working Protestant English and Scottish families into Ireland, you could either drive the existing shiftless, Catholic, Irish-speaking peasants off the valuable land and into the hills and bogs, or you could turn them

Map of Ireland 1558–1653, showing the patterns of political control

into decent, hard-working, civilised people, by providing good example. One way or another, God-fearing habits, laws, customs and religion could be permanently established. Ulster was the largest area colonised in this way, mainly by Scots.

It didn't, in the end, work out as expected. Not enough families wanted to uproot themselves to live in a foreign country full of untrustworthy natives. The people who did come were often profiteers, who didn't settle at all; they merely acquired large areas of Irish land in order to extract huge profits. Thousands of acres of Irish forest, for example, disappeared forever, sold as timber. Those families who did settle found that they could not do without the native Irish; they needed them as servants and to work the land, so complete segregation was not possible. Nor did the hoped-for changes in the Irish take place. Over previous centuries of colonisation, it was noted, incoming families had adopted the customs and society of their new homeland instead of the other way round – intermarrying, turning Catholic, learning to speak Irish, becoming 'more Irish than the Irish themselves' in the common phrase.

By the seventeenth century, Ireland was a society of several layers. The native Irish, dispossessed, and deeply resentful at having to work for those who now owned their land, were beneath the new emigrants. These were suspicious of the local Irish communities, while still needing them, and constantly kept themselves in a state of armed defence. Religion was even more divisive; Catholicism was seen by the incomers as a superstitious mumbo-jumbo suitable for ignorant peasants, and traitorous as well, because Catholics owed allegiance to the Pope in Rome, not to the king of England. There was also a layer of Anglo-Irish families who had come to Ireland centuries previously and made it their home, intermarrying with Gaelic-Irish ruling families. They owed allegiance to the English government and administration, and were known as the 'Old English'. But they were largely Catholic, and were therefore not safe from moves against them by the Protestant administration.

The 1641 Rebellion

The last Gaelic lords, Hugh O'Neill, Earl of Tyrone, and Hugh O'Donnell, Earl of Tyrconnell, left Ireland with their families in 1607, four years after the Nine Years' War ended. This event is known as 'The Flight of the Earls'. In Ireland, after that, there had been a certain acceptance of the Stuart dynasty as rulers, since they had a Scots Gaelic genealogy. The Reformation, however, had driven a wedge between the Irish and the Scots.

When the Stuart Charles I came to the throne in 1625, one of his sources of financial help was the Old English in Ireland. He promised them the 'Graces' – that is, tolerance for their Catholicism, and security that their property would not be confiscated – but he broke this promise when the wars against France and Spain ended, and he no longer needed their money. The Old English had dominated the Irish parliament in Dublin (which was independent from the English parliament at this time), but Charles' new Lord Deputy, Thomas Wentworth, Earl of Strafford, took charge of the administration in Dublin and managed to manipulate parliament for Charles' benefit. He suggested taking land for plantations from both Irish and Old English Catholics, and tried to recover former church property for the Church of Ireland, a move which was greatly resented by its new owners. He also began to raise an Irish army of about 8,000 foot soldiers and 1,000 cavalry to fight for the king. Some of the officers and most of the men of this army were Catholic.

When Charles ran into trouble with the Scots and with his own parliament, he had to agree to Wentworth's execution on charges of treason in May 1641. Wentworth was merely a scapegoat, and his execution was a warning signal to Charles. Parliament suspected that Charles had meant to use Wentworth's Irish army against his English subjects, and it was disbanded. The new administration in Ireland was more Puritan in composition than before, and the Old English grew nervous that the English parliament might join with the evangelical Scots to

Sir Thomas Wentworth, later Lord Strafford, with his secretary

...we wish we had no cause to speak of those insolencies, and savage usage and unheard of rapes, exercised upon our sex in Ireland, and have we not just cause to fear they will prove the forerunners of our ruin, except Almighty God by the wisdom and care of this parliament be pleased to succour us, our husbands and children ... our present fears are, that unless the blood-thirsty faction of the papists and prelates be hindered in their designs, ourselves here in England as well as they in Ireland, shall be exposed to that misery which is more intolerable than that which is already past, as namely to the rage not of men alone, but of devils incarnate, (as we may so say) besides the thraldom of our souls and consciences in matters concerning GOD, which of all things are most dear unto us...

Petition of London gentlewomen
and tradesmen's wives to parliament, 1642

suppress Catholicism completely. They began to come together with the native Irish, who still dreamed of regaining their rights. A plan for rebellion was hatched.

The plans were discovered and betrayed in Dublin, but uprisings did take place in other areas of the country. Thousands of English and Scottish settlers were stripped of everything and driven from their homes to die. It is estimated that about 8,000 died of cold and exposure, and about 4,000 were murdered. It was a vicious outburst of violence among individuals and neighbours who were well known to one another. Settlers were tortured to reveal any money they had, and opportunities were taken to destroy evidence of debt (Church of Ireland clergymen, in particular, had been active moneylenders). Chapels were reclaimed for Catholicism, and Protestant corpses were dug up from the graveyards.

One hundred Protestants were murdered from Portadown bridge, and others were burned to death elsewhere. In retaliation, settlers joined together to inflict great slaughter on the rebels. Seven hundred Irish were killed near Lisburn, Co. Antrim. Catholic priests were later blamed for incitement, but in fact they often rescued Protestant prisoners, and tried to control the violence of the rebels.

The mainspring of the rebellion was in Ulster, led by Sir Phelim O'Neill. His forces insisted they were rising to protect the king from the parliament, and they called themselves the 'Catholic Army'. The signed royal warrant they displayed to prove the king's support was probably a forgery, but it did Charles I a great deal of damage at home, where he was already suspected of being soft on popery.

The Ulster rebels reached Louth and Meath, but were eventually pushed back by English reinforcements under the leadership of the Anglo-Irish Protestant Earl of Ormond. Other rebels took Kilkenny as well as large parts of Munster, and much of Connaught also rose. Eventually the rebels, although poorly armed and disunited, held the largest part of the country, and the

James Butler, later Duke of Ormond (from a painting by Sir Godfrey Keller)

administration did not have the military strength to conquer them completely. The Dublin administration's very brutal response to the rebellion had driven the Old English Catholics of the Pale into the arms of the rebels, although they would have preferred to support the existing system. However, all Catholics were now seen as untrustworthy, and the future was looking bleak even for Catholic landowners.

In England, accounts of the rising were horrific; it was said that thousands of Protestants had been massacred, with the utmost brutality, and stories spread wildly as hundreds of refugees fled back to England and Scotland. Cromwell, among others, believed the atrocity tales implicitly, and this was one of the forces driving him when he came to Ireland some years later. Charles now had to ask parliament for money to campaign in Ireland, but parliament was increasingly unwilling to trust him with the control of an army.

> *Some of the persons particularly mentioned to have suffered, who are known unto you, are, Master German, minister of Brides, his body mangled, and his members cut off, Master Fullerton minister of Lughall, Simon Hastings, his ears cut off, Master Blandry minister, hanged, his flesh pulled off from his bones, in the presence of his wife, in small pieces, he being hanged two days before her, in the place where she is now prisoner. Abraham James of Newtown in the diocese of Clogher, cut in pieces....*
>
> *Letter from Thomas Partington, read in parliament,*
> *14 December 1641*

Confederation of Kilkenny

The rising of 1641 provided an ideal opportunity for the English government to assert its authority in Ireland, and plans were laid for large-scale confiscations of land. An Adventurers Act in 1642 promised land to those who lent money for the war in Ireland, and 2,500,000 acres were to be set aside for this purpose. As it happened, much of the money raised was actually used by parliament to fight the civil war in England, but this made no difference to the adventurers, who were still owed the land they had been promised.

Owen Roe O'Neill, 'that very brave and noble Irish cheiftain', according to the Pope (from a contemporary painting)

The Synod of Kells — which was presided over by the Archbishop of Armagh, Dr O'Reilly, in March 1642 — declared the support of the Catholic Church for the rising. The bishops said it was a just war, and advised that some sort of guiding council should be established. In May of that year, a provisional government of both churchmen and laymen, was set up in Kilkenny, and decided to put plans in place for a long-term war. This government, made up of the confederated Catholics of Ireland, was later called 'The Confederation of Kilkenny'. The aim of the provisional government was to try to regain the initiative and ultimately to take control of the uprising.

An oath of association was drawn up which vowed loyalty to the monarchy, but called for the free exercise of the Catholic faith. The provisional council was headed by Lord Mountgarrett, a grand-uncle of James Butler, Earl of Ormond, who controlled the Dublin parliament's army. A general council and four provincial councils were set up as well as separate military commands for Ulster, Munster, Leinster and Connaught.

The Confederation of Kilkenny was not a united body, although its motto was *'Pro Deo, rege et patria Hiberni unanimes'* (For God, King and Country, the Irish united). The bishops involved were strong supporters of the Counter-Reformation and of the authority of the Papacy, having been trained on the Continent. To them, Catholicism and Irishness were one and the same thing, and they were working towards a completely Catholic source of authority. However, the lay Confederates seem to have been more interested in the idea of an inclusive national identity. One delegate said in 1644, 'He that is born in Ireland, though his parents and all his ancestors were aliens, nay if his parents are Indians and Turks, if converted to Christianity, is an Irishman as fully as if his ancestors were born here for thousands of years and by the laws of England, as capable of the liberties of a subject.'

The Old English were reluctant rebels, driven by the fear of land confiscation, and they were anxious to settle with the king. Those of the native Irish who had little to lose were determined to fight on for as long as possible, but the landed Irish were worried about land confiscation as well. A group of non-aligned moderates tried to hold the Confederation together. The disunion among the Confederation in fact had more to do with social status than with race or religion. The Catholic landed élite did not want the existing plantations to be overturned, as most of them would then lose what they owned; they simply wanted to prevent new plantations.

The Confederation's forces were untrained and short of supplies. Military leadership was confused and inexperienced at first, but Irish exiles returned from the Continent to lead the war. They brought troops from abroad, and their own considerable experience of fighting in Europe's wars. France, which had seven Irish regiments in its army in 1641, had only one left by 1645. One of these returned exiles was Owen Roe O'Neill, nephew of the Earl of Tyrone, who was made general of the Ulster army. A great rival of O'Neill's, Thomas Preston, was made general in Leinster, but he and O'Neill never worked together successfully, and few of the native Irish landholders in Ulster supported O'Neill; he was seen as an outsider. He was appalled by the state of the country he had come to help, saying: 'Donegal not only looks like a desert, but like Hell, if there can be a Hell upon earth; for besides the sterility, destruction and bad condition it is in, the people are so rough and barbarous and miserable that many of them are little better in their ways than the most remote Indians.'

The Confederation's opponents were not united either. As civil war loomed, the English and Scottish Protestants in Ireland naturally began to take sides in the struggle between king and parliament. The Earl of Ormond, commander of the army, was a royalist, but most members of the Irish parliament were not. Charles tried desperately to make peace with the Confederation of Kilkenny, so that he could take Ormond's army of English and Welsh troops back for use in England. The only major battle fought against the Confederation had been a victory for Ormond at New Ross, Co. Wexford, in March 1643. Otherwise, the war was one of minor skirmishes and inconclusive sieges. Ormond's troops, while better trained, were extremely short of money and supplies. Even so, his army was costing £600,000 a year – seven times the annual income of Ireland.

The Confederates sent appeals to various continental countries whose sympathy they counted on, but they got little in return. The Pope sent money, supplies and an envoy. Spain and France also sent envoys, but were more interested in recruiting Irish mercenaries for their own wars. The Confederation began thinking about a truce, so that terms could be discussed. The

Irish parliament was not interested in a truce; instead, its members were convinced that the Confederates could be defeated easily. Ormond, however, was determined to take this chance of ending the war, so that he could go back to England and help Charles.

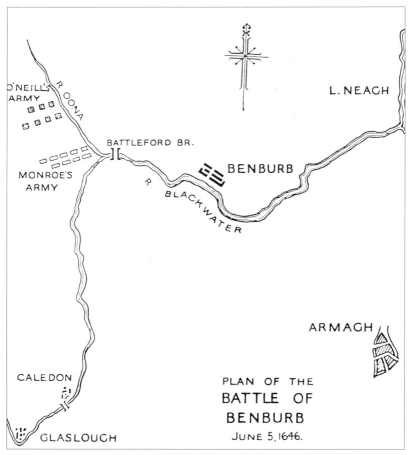

The Battle of Benburb, 5 June 1646, where O'Neill's army clashed with Monro (from D'Alton's History of Ireland*)*

A truce for one year was signed, and the Confederates agreed to pay Charles a sum of about £20,000. Immediately, 2,500 royalist troops were sent back to England, weakening the Irish parliament's position. Ormond was made Lord Lieutenant. The truce and Ormond's appointment were condemned by the English parliament. The Ulster Protestants, under the leadership of Major-General Munro, rejected the truce and continued the war. In Munster Lord Inchiquin ('Murrough of the Burnings'), who was Irish and Protestant, had joined the parliamentarians against the royalist side, and did not accept the truce either.

The Confederation sent delegates to the king in Oxford, to work out a final peace. They wanted freedom of religion for Catholics, and Old English control of the Irish parliament. But Irish Protestants also arrived in Oxford, demanding anti-Catholic laws, and Protestant control of the Irish parliament. Charles made no commitments, but authorised Ormond to negotiate for him. These negotiations dragged on for two years, all through the civil war. Meanwhile a new pope, Innocent X, was elected in Rome, and appointed to Ireland a Papal Nuncio with powers of excommunication.

After his defeat in the battle of Naseby, in 1645, Charles was even more anxious to agree terms, but Ormond would not give the Confederates the freedom of religion they were holding out for. Charles decided he needed someone more flexible to negotiate for him, and chose the Earl of Glamorgan, a Catholic. Without Ormond's knowledge, Glamorgan organised another treaty, offering complete freedom to Catholics, and land and property rights to the Catholic Church. An army of 10,000 Confederates was to be provided for the king.

It is possible Charles himself did not know what had been promised. When the provisions of the treaty were revealed accidentally, he was acutely embarrassed, and protested he had known nothing about the terms. He was widely disbelieved. The Confederates held out to see if these favourable terms would be repeated, but Ormond was not going to go down that road, and a different agreement was made in March 1646. Again, 10,000 soldiers would be sent to England, and various concessions were made on Catholic disabilities. However, Archbishop Giovanni Battista Rinuccini, the Papal Nuncio who had been sent to the Confederation in October 1645, now entered the game.

Rinuccini threatened to excommunicate anyone who accepted this new treaty, because it did not stand firm for the full rights of the Catholic Church to freedom of worship and ownership of property. Some months later Owen Roe O'Neill won a great victory over Munro's Scots at Benburb, near Armagh, on 5 June 1646, and then marched to support Rinuccini instead of following up his advantage in Ulster. In September, Rinuccini and O'Neill entered Kilkenny, and deposed and imprisoned the supreme council of the Confederation. The truce was over.

Rinuccini's behaviour was seen as arrogant, and support slipped further from him as O'Neill and Preston failed to take Dublin. He released the supreme council of the Confederation from prison and called a general assembly for January 1647. The 1645 treaty was repudiated again, but negotiations still continued with Ormond, although it was obvious he would never offer enough to satisfy Rinuccini. Ormond himself, realising there was little point in this, and that Charles' cause was lost, finally handed over all the garrisons in his control to parliamentary troops from England. He felt it was better to leave the army to the parliament rather than to Catholics. Leaving Ireland in July 1647, Ormond joined Queen Henrietta Maria and the Prince of Wales in exile in France.

> *What really surprises the majority of those who contemplate the affairs of Ireland is to see that people of the same nation and of the same religion — who are well aware that the resolution to exterminate them totally has already been taken — should differ so strongly in their private hostilities; that their zeal for religion, the preservation of their country and their own self-interest are not sufficient to make them lay down, at least for a short time, the passions which divide them one from the other.*
>
> *French ambassador to England, 1648*

The new parliamentary commander, Michael Jones, using Ormond's troops, defeated Preston, and Inchiquin took back almost all of Munster for the parliament. When the Confederate general assembly met again in November, bruised by these defeats, the Old English were in a majority over the Gaelic Irish, and they appointed a new supreme council. They then negotiated a truce with Inchiquin, and this was instantly condemned by Rinuccini. The council appealed to Rome for a judgment, and dismissed O'Neill as Ulster general because of his support for the cardinal. He was proclaimed traitor.

Light horseman of the New Model Army, the storm troopers of the Parliamentary faction

Rinuccini, now powerless, left Ireland in early 1649. Inchiquin changed allegiance back to the king, against the parliament. The Ulster Scots also became more inclined to the royalist cause. A new royalist alliance seemed on the cards, and Ormond arrived back in Ireland to assist it. The Confederation had been weakened by its inability to choose between supporting Charles, hoping he would win, and relying on foreign support to help fight off English aggression. Another truce was signed, and the Confederation of Kilkenny was dissolved in early 1649. Twelve commissioners were then appointed as a replacement 'government'.

Charles I had just been executed; royalists now pledged their faith to Charles, Prince of Wales. Ormond hoped that the horror of the execution would bring more support to his side. But O'Neill, not interested in co-operating with Ormond, had come to terms with the parliamentary forces in Ulster by himself. Michael Jones refused to negotiate with Ormond at all. A new phase of the war began. Inchiquin won Dundalk for the parliament, and drove Monck, the Ulster commander-in-chief, from Drogheda. Ormond failed to take Dublin. He was attacked by Michael Jones at Rathmines, near the city, on 2 August 1649, and was completely overwhelmed. He escaped to Kilkenny.

As for the pleasures of this life and outward business, let that be upon the bye. Be above all these things, by faith in Christ, and then you shall have the true use and comfort of them, and not otherwise.... The Lord is very near, which we see by His wonderful works, and therefore He looks that we of this generation draw near Him. This late great mercy of Ireland is a great manifestation thereof. Your husband will acquaint you with it. We should be much stirred up in our spirits to thankfulness. We much need the spirit of Christ to enable us to praise God for so admirable a mercy.

Letter from Cromwell to his daughter-in-law about Ormond's defeat, written while sailing to Ireland

---

The end of the war was in sight, following the royalists' great losses. At this point, Oliver Cromwell arrived in Ireland for what would be more a mopping-up operation than the full-scale war he had been expecting.

The Seal of the Confederation of Kilkenny

According to The Moderate Intelligencer

This evening, about five of the clock,
The Lord Protector set out for Ireland
In a coach with six gallant Flanders mares
And a life-guard consisting of eighty men:
Ireton, Scroop, Horton, Lambert,
Abbott, Mercer, Fletcher, Garland,
Bolton, Ewer, Cooke, Hewson,
Jones, Monk, Deane. And others.
May God bring Cromwell safe to Dublin
To propagate the Gospel of Christ
Among the barbarous, bloodthirsty Irish
Whose cursing, swearing, drunken ways
Dishonour God by sea and land.
Visit them, Oliver, like God's right hand.

Brendan Kennelly, Cromwell *(Bloodaxe Books, 1987)*

3: Cromwell in Ireland

Oliver Cromwell, the new Lord Lieutenant of Ireland, landed with his army at Ringsend, Dublin, on 15 August 1649. He had been extremely seasick on the journey across the Irish Sea. He seems to have been in poor health at this time, and had, unusually, brought a doctor with him. After landing, he made a speech about the great peace and prosperity there had once been in Ireland, and how this had been grievously and wantonly disturbed by the rising of 1641 and the subsequent war. He came, he said, 'for the propagating of the Gospel of Christ, the establishing of truth and peace'.

He issued an official declaration that his soldiers would not rob or do violence to civilians, and would pay for anything they required while in Ireland. He had taken precautions to ensure proper supplies and equipment for his army, and their pay was up to date. Until then, parliamentary forces in Ireland had been poorly supplied; Sir Charles Cook wrote from Londonderry in June 1647 that many of his troops had died 'for want of bread to sustain nature'.

> *[Ireland is] capable of being governed by such laws as should be found most agreeable to justice, which may be so impartially administered as to be a good precedent even to England itself; where when they once perceive property preserved at an easy and cheap rate in Ireland they will never permit themselves to be so cheated and abused as now they are.*
>
> *Cromwell to Edmund Ludlow, member of Council of State*

The English government was extremely concerned about the unsettled state of Ireland. It would be an obvious source of support for the young Prince of Wales if he landed in Scotland, as it was feared he would do. So this was to be a short, sharp campaign, a form of surgery to remove disease as quickly as possible. Of course, it was not just a crusade for the Lord, or for England's security. Vast confiscations of land and property were about to take place, and huge profits would be made from them. However, Cromwell also seems to have seen Ireland (once the natives were cleared out) as an opportunity to build a decent society, with a proper legal system and equality before the law, where policies could be tested before they were introduced in England. Civilised settlers would be brought in, and peace would reign.

> *We have a great opportunity to set up, until the Parliament shall otherwise determine, a way of doing justice amongst these poor people, which, for the uprightness and cheapness of it, may exceedingly gain upon them, who have been accustomed to as much injustice, tyranny and oppression from their landlords, the great men, and those that should have done them right as, I believe, any people in that which we call Christendom.*
>
> *Cromwell to his friend John Sadler, Dec 1649*
> *(offering him the position of Chief Justice of Munster)*

To the English, the Irish had always seemed both primitive and barbaric. Not just their religion but their customs and manners were alien. Not all the English were of this opinion however; the army Levellers, who had refused to be sent to Ireland, stated: 'The cause of the Irish natives in seeking their just freedoms was

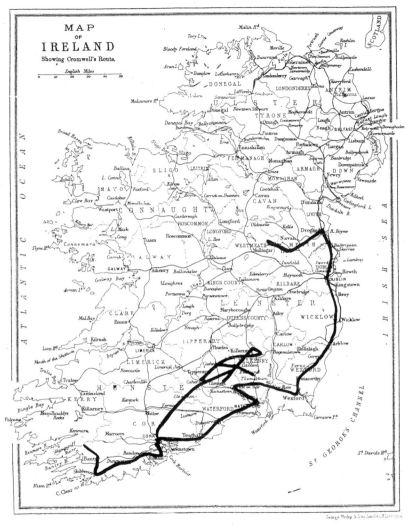

Map of Ireland, showing Cromwell's route in 1649

the very same with our cause here in endeavouring our own res-
cue and freedom from the power of oppressors'. Cromwell shared
the prejudices of most of his countrymen. He did not see the
Irish as human beings on a level with himself; they were much
lower on the scale, and were not necessarily to be treated as
civilised enemies, by the accepted rules of war.

In Scotland, the campaign had been as much for 'hearts and
minds' as for military victory. This was not relevant in Ireland,
because the Irish had no hearts or minds that Cromwell could be
interested in. Catholics were not persecuted in England under
the Commonwealth, but in Ireland, the Catholic Church was a
political as well as a religious force, and Cromwell was determined to destroy it if he could. As he said, 'I had rather be
overrun with a Cavalierish interest, than a Scotch interest; I had
rather be overrun with a Scotch interest than an Irish interest;
and I think of all this is most dangerous.... All the world knows
their barbarism.'

He was facing a motley collection of royalist forces under the
command of Ormond, who was now in Meath. Inchiquin was
leading a Protestant royalist army in Munster, Clanricard led a
Catholic royalist army in Connaught, and Owen Roe O'Neill had
decided, after the disaster of the battle of Rathmines, that he
would go into battle for the royalist cause again. None of these
armies was strong enough to face Cromwell's troops on the battle-
field, even if they united, but among them they held almost all
the fortified towns in the country. This was going to be a war
of sieges. Most of the ports, however, were held by the
Commonwealth, so Cromwell's lines of communication were
kept open.

Drogheda

Cromwell's first objective was the town of Drogheda in County
Louth, a gateway to Ulster. It was under the command of Sir
Arthur Aston, who had fought for Charles in England; he had
2,200 foot soldiers and 320 cavalry. Cromwell's forces consisted of

8,000 foot soldiers and 4,000 cavalry but, more importantly, he also had eleven siege-guns as well as twelve pieces of field artillery.

Contemporary woodcut of massacres in Ireland

Drogheda, which was surrounded by a town wall, was in a very strong defensive position, even though its harbour had been blockaded. Sir Arthur boasted that 'The man who could take Drogheda could take hell'. His job was to delay Cromwell as long as possible. If he kept the siege going, the English army might begin to run short of food, or to fall ill in their exposed camp – Ormond was a great believer in 'Colonel Hunger' and 'Major Sickness'. Aston relied heavily on the fact that to the south of the town was a hill which would have to be overcome by any attackers. At one corner of this hill stood a church, St Mary's, and the steeple gave defenders a clear view, very useful to snipers. Beyond this again was the Mill Mount, a high artificial mound. There was no other direction by which the town could be entered.

Cromwell called on Drogheda to surrender, and Aston refused. Now, it was very clear to all concerned what this meant, by contemporary rules of war. If a town refused to surrender and forced its enemies to besiege it, no mercy or 'quarter' would be given to the defending troops if they were overcome in the end. Because sieges were so wasteful of time and manpower, the aim was to avoid them as far as possible, and the threat of massive slaughter was a real one. The rules of war were designed for armies, of course, not civilians, but a besieged town would inevitably be full of civilians, who would have nowhere else to go.

On 10 September, Cromwell's cannons beat down the church steeple and breached the walls, but his troops were driven back. On 11 September they charged the church again, and finally, after a third assault under Cromwell himself, it was seized. It seems at this stage that quarter was offered, unexpectedly, to some of the officers and men who laid down their arms but this was never officially made clear. Certainly, Cromwell was in no mood to offer it; he had fallen into one of the rages which occasionally possessed him.

The men seem to have been overwhelmed with their commander's passion, and pursued the defenders, mostly English Royalist troops, through the narrow streets, killing all before them. Some attempt may have been made to avoid civilian deaths, but priests were another matter, and every priest seen was killed. In the church of St Peter's, to the north of Drogheda, dozens of people crowded into the steeple for shelter; a fire was set below them and they burned to death as if they were in a chimney. In all, about 3,000 were officially said to have died in Drogheda, but the official calculations probably only include military casualties. Parliament called a day of thanksgiving for 30 October to celebrate this great victory.

> *'Not long afterwards came Colonel Hewson and told the Doctor he had orders to blow up the steeple (which stood between the choir and the body of the church), where about threescore men were run up for refuge, but the three barrels of powder which he had caused to be put under it for that end blew up only the body of the church. The same night, Hewson caused the seats of the church to be broken up, and made a great pile of them under the steeple, which, firing it, took the lofts wherein five great bells hung, and from thence it flamed up to the top, and so at once men and bells and roof came all down together, the most hideous sight and terrible cry that ever he was a witness of at once....*
>
> *Account of Nicholas Bernard,*
> *Dean of St Peter's, Drogheda*

Contemporary woodcut
of massacres in Ireland

By The Lord Lieutenant Generall of Ireland.

WHEREAS I am informed that the horfe vnder my Commande (fince their being quartered within the *Black-water*) have and doe in their feverall quarters take away and waft Wheate and Barly for their horfes ; And doe behave themfelves outrageoufly towards the Inhabitants not contenting themfelves with fuch Provifions as they are able to afforde them , but doe kill their fheepe and other cattle within and as often as they pleafe. I doe hereby ftraightly charge and Commande all Souldiers to forbeare fuch like practices upon paine of Death. And whereas fuch offences as thefe cannot be comitted without the confent , connivance or at leaft the negleft of the Officers , I doe hereby require them as they will anfwer it at their vtmoft perills That they be diligent in governeing the Souldiers vnder their commands in their carriage to the Inhabitants in this Province of *Mounfter* in fubjeftion to the Parliament , According to the Articles , Rules , and Difcipline of War exercife in the Army, in the Army in *England* towards the Inhabitants there. And I doe hereby farther declare that if any Inhabitant within the lymitts aforefaid fhall make his greivance knowne unto the Officer of any of the refpeftive Souldiers that fhall doe any wrong as aforefaid and the faid Officer upon proofe made fhall refufe to doe the faid party right , that then the faid party makeing complaint to me fhall have fatisfaftion for his damage from the faid Officer. And I doe farther will and require all Officers and Souldiry within the lymitts aforefaid , that they doe not breake downe any ftackes of Barly or Wheate in their refpative quarters , to give the fame to their horfes ; But that they content themfelves with Peafe , Oates , Hay , and fuch other forrage as the Country afords paying or giving Ticketts at fuch reafonable Rates for the fame, as they were vfually fold for , before their comeing into the faid quarters. Given under my hande this 8. day of December 1649.

O. CROMWELL

Above: Cromwell in Cork: a proclamation

Left: Portrait of Oliver Cromwell with Dublin in the background

Above*: The Siege of Drogheda: Cromwell and his officers before the city (Ken Neill)*

Below: Cromwell's massacre at Drogheda. (Courtesy Central Catholic Library)

Above: Cromwell's Fort, Drogheda, from a nineteenth-century woodcut.

Left: St Laurence's Gate, in Drogheda, one of only two left standing after the siege in 1649.

> *Divers of the enemy retreated into the 'Mill Mount', a place very strong, and of difficult access, being exceedingly high, having a good graft, and strongly palisadoed. The Governor, Sir Arthur Ashton, and divers considerable officers being there, our men getting up to them, they were ordered by me to put them all to the sword, and indeed being in the heat of action, I forbid them to spare any that were in arms in the town, and I think that night they put to the sword about 2,000 men.... From one of the said towers, notwithstanding their condition, they killed and wounded some of our men. When they submitted themselves, their officers were knocked on the head, and every tenth man of the soldiers killed, and the rest shipped for the Barbadoes.*
>
> *Cromwell reporting from Drogheda, 17 September 1649*

Whether Cromwell intended such slaughter is not certain; he had not tried to pull his men back. He was pleased, at any rate, that such an example of ruthlessness meant he was not likely to have to face many more sieges. He wrote, 'It will tend to prevent the effusion of blood for the future, which are the satisfactory grounds to such actions, which otherwise cannot but work remorse and regret.' Other towns would probably surrender at once, in fear of a repeat.

In the letter he wrote to parliament announcing the end of the siege and the massacre of its defenders, Cromwell made no reference to civilian casualties. This could mean that there were not many such casualties, and that stories of the sack of Drogheda have been wildly exaggerated over the years, as useful propaganda for the Irish side. However, it is equally possible that he was not interested in recording 'collateral damage'; a commander's job is to report on his troops and how they fought against other troops. Civilians might get in the way, but are ultimately irrelevant.

This disaster for the Irish had the desired effect. The towns of Trim and Dundalk put up no resistance at all, and Newry, Carlingford and Belfast fell to Colonel Robert Venables. Cromwell turned back to Dublin to greet his wife, who had just arrived, then proceeded south. On 1 October, the Cromwellian forces, by this time consisting of 7,000 foot and 2,000 horse, drew up in front of Wexford town.

Wexford

Winter had begun, and Cromwell's army was beginning to suffer the consequences. It was necessary to find shelter, and Wexford was the obvious place for winter quarters (fighting always came to a halt during the winter months). Within Wexford the military leader, Colonel David Sinnott, and the civilian population were at loggerheads. The townspeople wanted to surrender peacefully, but Sinnott refused, and prepared for a siege. He was fairly hopeful about this; the town was surrounded by a massive wall, and the harbour was still open, so he might receive reinforcements from Ormond before long. When, therefore, Cromwell called on the town to surrender, Sinnott delayed, suggesting a truce on honourable terms. Reinforcements did arrive for Sinnott, under Lord Castlehaven, and they both asked for more time to consider terms.

After three days Cromwell, angry at the delay, placed his guns on high ground above the town. Ormond then appeared, sending 500 foot and 100 cavalry into Wexford. Sinnott continued negotiating. Cromwell agreed to the free departure of soldiers who promised not to bear arms against parliament in the future, and said he would protect the town's citizens from plunder. Things were going well for a settlement, but a young man called Captain Stafford decided to betray the defensive castle to Cromwell. The castle was built up against the town walls, so Cromwell's men were then able to climb over these walls and storm the town.

No-one was quite sure later what had happened, but it seems clear from various accounts that Cromwell's soldiers completely lost control, and a massacre took place. Not one of Cromwell's officers seems to have tried to stop them, nor did Cromwell himself. Again, priests were particularly singled out, and it seems that 1,500 civilians died, quite apart from the English royalist defenders.

> ...*[the army] ran violently upon the town with their ladders, and stormed it. And when they were come into the market-place, the enemy making stiff resistance, our forces brake them, and then put all to the sword that came in their way. Two boatfuls of the enemy attempting to escape, being overprest with numbers sank, whereby were drowned near three hundred of them. I believe, in all, there was lost of the enemy not many less than two thousand; and I believe not twenty of yours killed from first to last of the siege.*
>
> Cromwell, reporting on Wexford

Cromwell said in his report that God had brought 'a righteous judgement' on Wexford, but he regretted that the destruction of the town had been so complete: 'I could have wished for their own good, and the good of the garrison, they had been more moderate.' Wexford town was no longer in a fit state for winter quarters, so the Cromwellian army moved on to the town of New Ross, which surrendered.

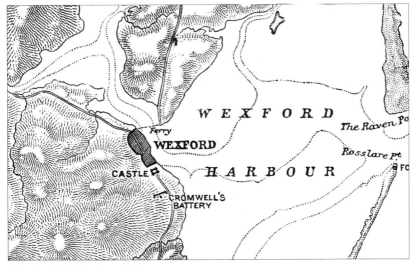

Wexford, 2–11 October 1649

At New Ross Cromwell fell ill, possibly with a recurrence of the malarial sickness he suffered from. He was depressed and wrote gloomy letters to his family, but he had no need for gloom. Owen Roe O'Neill had died, after a long illness. The garrison in Cork had revolted against its royalist commander, and declared for the Commonwealth. Youghal, Cappoquin and Mallow followed Cork, and even Lord Inchiquin seemed to be ready to make terms.

> *This town is now so in your power, that [of] the former inhabitants, I believe scarce one in twenty can challenge any property in their houses. Most of them are run away, and many of them killed in this service. And it were to be wished that an honest people would come and plant here, where are very good houses, and other accommodations fitted to their hands, and may by your favour be made of encouragement to them, as also a seat of good trade, both inward and outward, and of marvellous great advantage in the point of herring and other fishing. This town is pleasantly seated and strong, having a rampart of earth within the wall, near fifteen foot thick.*
>
> Cromwell, reporting on Wexford

In late November the Cromwellian army moved on to Waterford, which refused to surrender. The army by this time was suffering from its exposure to an Irish winter, and as many as 1,000 are thought to have died from fevers. Abandoning Waterford, Cromwell moved on to Youghal in County Cork and settled his army into winter quarters at long last. On the journey Colonel Michael Jones had died, 'having run his course with so much honour, courage and fidelity, as his actions speak better than my pen,' Cromwell wrote.

Cromwell was extremely annoyed by a statement issued by the Catholic bishops after a conference at Clonmacnoise, on 4 December, which proclaimed a kind of holy war (its stridently Catholic tone also alienated Anglo-Irish Protestant royalists). He responded with a vicious Declaration, attacking the Irish for their slaughter of innocent Protestants in 1641, and condemning the Catholic Church for inciting peaceful civilians to horrid crimes. He wrote:

> Remember, ye hypocrites, Ireland was once united to England.... You broke this union! You, unprovoked, put the English to the most unheard-of and most barbarous massacre (without respect of sex or age) that ever the sun beheld.... Is God, will God be, with you? I am confident He will not.

He promised that this would not remain unpunished:

> We are come to ask an account of the innocent blood that hath been shed.... We come (by the assistance of God) to hold forth and maintain the lustre and glory of English liberty in a nation where we have an undoubted right to do it....'

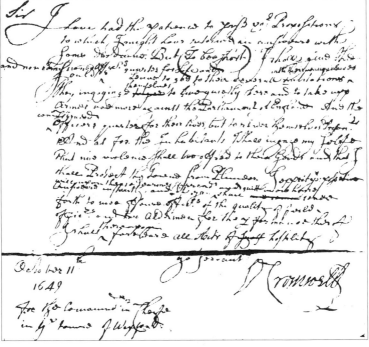

Cromwell to the Governor of Wexford, offering terms

Surrender of Irish Fortresses 1649–1652

Ross	Surrendered to Cromwell	19 October 1649
Cork	Corporation of, proposals to Cromwell	November 1649
Bandon	Town, proposition to deliver it up to Lord Broghill	15 November 1649
Cahir	Castle, surrendered to Cromwell	24 February 1649
Kilkenny	City and Castle surrendered to Cromwell	27 March 1650
Protestant Delinquents	Under Marquis of Ormonde. Articles of protection from Cromwell	26 April 1650
Clonmel	Town and garrison. Articles of agreement with Cromwell	18 May 1650
Fethard	Town and garrison. Articles of agreement with Cromwell	No date
Athlone	Castle of, surrendered to Sir Charles Coote	18 June 1651
Galway	Town, surrendered	5 April 1652
Jamestown	Articles of surrender	7 April 1652
Drumruske	Articles of surrender	8 April 1652
Clare	Brigade, surrender of	21 April 1652
Dromagh	Surrendered	23 May 1652
Ballyshannon	Surrendered	26 May 1652
Newtown	Fort of, surrendered	3 June 1652
Ross Islands	Surrendered to Ludlow	22 June 1652
Ballymote	Surrendered	24 June 1652
Mullagh	Surrendered	28 June 1652
Clanricarde	Conditions granted to him on leaving Ireland	28 June 1652
Connaught	Irish forces of, with Lord President of Connaught. Articles of agreement on laying down their arms	14 July 1652
Inchilogher	Surrendered to Colonel Sankey	14 August 1652
Kilkenny	Surrender of Irish armies of Leinster, Ulster, Munster and Connaught, to Lt-General Ludlow, Commander-in-Chief of the Parliamentary Forces	15 January 1652
	Fort of, in Arran, surrendered	15 January 1652
Innisboffyn	Island, surrendered on conditions	14 February 1652
Ballyleague	Fort, surrendered to Commissary-General Reynolds	24 February 1652

4: The Cromwellian Settlement

Cromwell Leaves Ireland

Marching season began again in late January, and this time Cromwell's forces headed for Munster. The castles of Cahir, Cashel and Fethard surrendered, and were granted mercy. Cromwell joined forces with his son-in-law, Henry Ireton, and turned towards Kilkenny, which was held for Ormond by Sir Walter Butler. After two attacks had failed, Butler proposed terms, which were accepted, and his army was allowed to leave unmolested, leaving most of its weapons behind. Cromwell had promised his army that the town would pay to avoid being sacked, and a sum of £2,000 was handed over as ransom.

By now it was April, and Cromwell was receiving urgent messages from home. The situation in Scotland was deteriorating, and parliament needed its war leader badly. The Clonmacnoise document had done its work of alienating Protestant royalists, and the royalist opposition was beginning to melt away. Ormond quarrelled with the Catholic bishops, and they released all Catholics from any duty to obey him. Meanwhile the Prince of

Wales, who needed Scottish support, had been forced to deny any contact with the 'Irish rebels', including his royalist supporters in Ireland; Ormond had been betrayed. Some royalist troops negotiated their own disbandment, on condition that they went abroad rather than to England, and Lady Ormond and her family were given a safe conduct to leave Ireland.

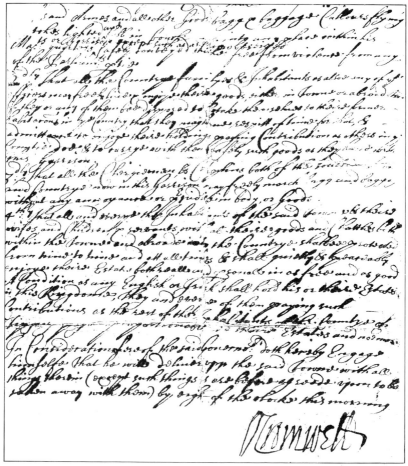

Extract from the agreement made between Cromwell and Piers Butler for the surrender of Fethard

Cromwell now turned his attention to Clonmel, which was being held by Hugh O'Neill, nephew of Owen Roe, with 1,200 men. O'Neill blocked the narrow streets behind the town walls, so that when Cromwell's men came over the walls they found themselves caught in traps and cut to pieces. Up to 2,000 are said to have died. The army retreated, after a second fruitless assault. O'Neill knew that Cromwell would win in the end, so he laid plans to escape. The mayor of Clonmel began negotiations, and terms were agreed for safe conduct and protection for the defenders. Cromwell, entering the town, found that O'Neill and his men had vanished over the walls the night before. He was furious that he had been tricked, but he kept the terms that had been agreed. This was one of the very few defeats he suffered.

...And now the Irish are ashamed
To see themselves in one year tamed:
So much one man can do,
That does both act and know.
They can affirm his praises best,
And have, though overcome, confessed
How good he is, how just,
And fit for highest trust:
Nor yet grown stiffer with command,
But still in the Republic's hand:
How fit he is to sway
That can so well obey....

'An Horatian Ode upon Cromwell's return from Ireland'
Andrew Marvell (1621–78)

On 26 May 1650, Oliver Cromwell took ship from Youghal and sailed back to England, never to see Ireland again. He left the campaign under the care of Henry Ireton as commander-in-chief. Ireton finally managed to take Waterford in August, and Limerick the following year after a six-month siege, but he died, possibly of plague, in November 1651. His widow, Cromwell's daughter Bridget, married Charles Fleetwood, the new commander in Ireland.

Great numbers of people endeavoured to get out of the town, sent out by the garrison either as useless persons or to spread the contagion amongst us [plague]. The Deputy [Ireton] commanded them to retire, and threatened to shoot any that should come out for the future; but this not being sufficient to make them desist, he caused two or three to be taken out in order to be executed, and the rest to be whipped back into the town. One of those that were to be hanged was the daughter of an old man, who was in that number which was to be sent back; he desired that he might be hanged in the room of his daughter, but that was refused, and he with the rest driven back into the town. After which a gibbet was erected in the sight of the town walls, and one or two persons hanged up who had been condemned for other crimes, and by this means they were so terrified that we were no farther disturbed on that account.

Edmund Ludlow on the siege of Limerick

Ormond had left Ireland in December 1650, with Inchiquin and other royalist leaders. (After Charles II's restoration in 1660, Ormond returned to Ireland as Duke of Ormond and Lord Lieutenant.) Command of the royalist forces was now delegated to the Earl of Clanricard. The last of the Irish cities to fall to the Commonwealth was Galway, which surrendered in May 1652 to Edmund Ludlow and Charles Fleetwood, and Clanricard himself surrendered in June.

By the end of the war, 34,000 royalist soldiers had been sent into exile, and 10,000 more transported to the West Indies as prisoners of war, to act as indentured servants or bondsmen.

The Cromwellian Settlement

The Adventurers Act of March 1642 had offered 2,500,000 acres, in all four provinces of Ireland, in return for financial sub-scriptions. 1,533 'adventurers' had subscribed at the time, paying over £306,718, but by 1650 the number of people interested in this

Oliver Cromwell at his Farm at St Ives, 1630, *by Ford Madox Brown (1874). Here is Cromwell as the bluff English yeoman about to answer the call of the nation to save it from perdition*

(Courtesy of National Museums and Galleries on Merseyside)

Cromwell at the Storming of Basing House, *by Ernest Crofts (1900).*
A pivotal point in the first civil war in 1645. This is Cromwell as the
farmer turned military man

(Courtesy of Leeds City Art Gallery/The Bridgeman Art Library)

Above: *Battle re-enactor dressed in Cromwellian-period costume*

(Courtesy of the English Heritage Photographic Library)

Cromwell with Charles I and his children, *by Daniel Maclise (1836)*

(Courtesy of the National Gallery of Ireland)

Above: Charles I on his way to Execution,
by Ernest Crofts (1883).
*Charles faced his death with calm resolution, but
afterwards these trees were cut down and
destroyed for fear that Royalists would clip them
away as relics of a king whom some saw as a
martyr for the Anglican faith*

(From an oleograph published by
Messrs Hildesheimer, London)

Right: *Historical re-
enactment of the Siege
of Pendennis Castle*

(Courtesy of the
English Heritage
Photographic Library)

Above: Cromwell at the Battle of Dunbar, 1650,
by Andrew Carrick Gow (1886).
The victory over the Scots that finally ended the
civil wars and secured the Protectorate

Statue of Oliver Cromwell at the Houses of Parliament in London
(Courtesy of the British Tourist Authority)

project had dropped to 1,043. It had taken a long time to make Ireland 'safe for civilisation', and many of the original speculators were tired of waiting and sold their interest to others. Irish land had also been promised to up to 35,000 soldiers, instead of their pay. There was no actual money to pay their wages, so it was essential that the land should be available. Land for specific regiments was decided by lot, and each regiment was to be settled in one area only, so that the colonists would all know one another.

The triumphant Governor of Ireland on his return to London (Engraving by Mazot)

However, no-one knew exactly how much land was available for legal confiscation, or indeed how much land Ireland contained overall. A series of surveys began; the largest was the 'Down Survey' ('by survey laid down') carried out by the Physician-General William Petty, at a payment of £6 per 1,000 acres. This was not completed until 1659.

In 1652, an act was passed for the settlement of Ireland which concentrated more on punishment than anything else. If it had been fully carried out, almost half of the adult male population would have been executed. As it was, thousands went into exile. All persons of property were at risk; the whole point of the legislation was to seize as much land as possible. A high court was established to try those considered guilty of murder or treason, and several hundred were executed, but the court seems to have wound itself up by late 1654. Others found that their land was forfeit in exchange for their life, and were told that they would be given land elsewhere of one-third or two-thirds its value, depending on the degree of their guilt.

The Cromwellian Settlement posed an immense administrative problem. There could not be enough land in the whole island to fulfil all the claims on it. Anglo-Irish landowners who had been promised immunity suddenly found that they were out on the road with everyone else, and others who had been promised land in Connaught found their grants drastically reduced.

The plan was to clear the Catholic Irish off the land in three of the provinces, and move them to the remaining one. Connaught was chosen to be that province, although it was considered to contain richer and more valuable land than Ulster. It was felt that the dispossessed would be more or less prisoner there, trapped between the sea and the Shannon River, and would be less able to mount any kind of rebellion. Plans were also made to move the Scottish settlers in Ulster, resettling them among English proprietors, but these plans were not carried out. Once Scotland had been overcome, the Ulster Scots were no longer a threat. Presbyterian ministers were hunted out, however, and transported to Scotland.

> They are seated in a country furthest distant from England, and for the sea shore most remote from the course of the English fleet, where therefor they may receive arms from any foreign prince with most security, modelise themselves into arms and be furnished irresistibly for a new war, by means of these advantages, the English in the last rebellion first lost Connaught, and last regain'd it....
>
> ...they exceedingly mistake who imagine that the passage out of Connaught into the other three provinces is difficult, or may be easily defended against the Irish, if they should thus be armed and fitted for a new war.
>
> Vincent Gookin, Kinsale, pamphlet attacking
> transplantation policy (published anonymously), 1655

The original aim had been to transplant all native Irish and Anglo-Irish alike, landlords and tenants, but gradually a pattern emerged of transplanting only the landlords with their dependants. The tenants had to stay behind to work the land for its new

A   Ten counties divided out between the adventur-
    ers and the soldiers
B   County Louth additional security to the
    adventurers
C   Seven counties additional security to the soldiers
D   Parts of Connaught subsequently taken from
    what was reserved for the Irish as additional
    security for the soldiers who had fought in
    England during the Civil War
E   Four counties given up in 1654 for the arrears
    of pay due to the Munster garrison who had
    revolted from Inchiquin to Lord Broghill in
    1649
F   The parts of Connaught and Clare which were
    reserved for the Irish and which had a 1-mile
    line of soldiers planted to surround them
G   Four counties reserved by the Government

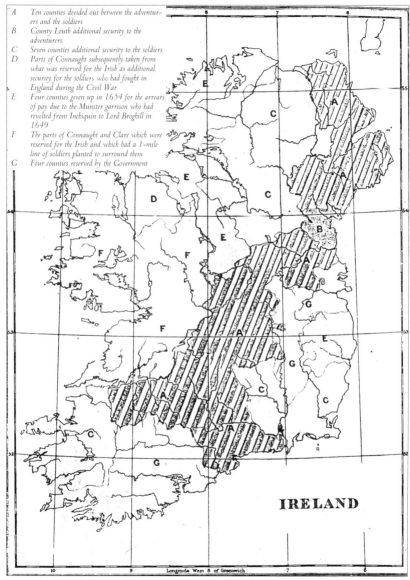

Map of the Cromwellian settlement (Courtesy of the Central Catholic Library)

owners, because the number of intending emigrants from England shrank month by month. Some few English adventurers were becoming the holders of enormous parcels of land by buying out the interest of soldiers who had no interest in moving to Ireland, or of speculators whose circumstances had changed in the years since they had made their original investment.

Before the Cromwellian Settlement took place, it has been calculated that Catholics owned 59 per cent of the land of Ireland (although this is possibly an overestimate). By 1660, they owned 20 per cent, mostly in Connaught. Of the 35,000 serving soldiers, 12,000 had moved to Ireland. They were settling in a devastated country, ruined by several years of war. Development of a market economy had been set back years, and famine had spread widely during the 1640s, as well as plague, smallpox and dysentery. Some areas had not done badly from the war, such as ports which continued to trade with the continent. Wexford's shipbuilding industry had flourished, for example.

Cromwell's armies had deliberately destroyed the land they passed through, and it took many years to recover. Pettys estimated the population at 850,000, of whom 160,000 were Protestants, but this total is seen by modern historians as far too low. He estimated that 616,000 had died since 1641. Descriptions survive of famished peasants eating grass, or starving on the roads, very close to descriptions of the Great Famine two hundred years later.

...the great multitude of poor swarming in all parts of the nation ... frequently some are found feeding on carrion and weeds and some starved in the highways, and many times poor children who have lost their parents, or who have been deserted by them, are found exposed to, and some of them fed upon by, ravening wolves and other beasts and birds of prey.

Commissioners [of Parliament] for Ordering and Settling the Affairs of Ireland, reporting in May, 1653

About the year 1652 and 1653 the plague and famine had so swept away whole counties that a man might travel twenty or thirty miles and not see a living creature, either man, beast or bird, they being either all dead or had quit those desolate places; or soldiers would tell stories of the place where they saw a smoke; it was so rare to see either smoke by day or fire or candle by night. And when we did meet with two or three poor cabins, none but very aged men and women and children, and those, like the prophet, might have complained: We are become as a bottle in the smoke; our skin is black like an oven, because of the terrible famine. I have seen those miserable creatures plucking stinking, rotten carrion out of a ditch, black and rotten, and been credibly informed that they dug corpses out of the grave to eat.

Col Richard Lawrence, governor of Waterford,
writing in 1655

...Upon consideration had of the multitude of persons, especially women and children wandering up and down the country, that daily perish in ditches, and are starved for want of relief: it is thought fit that such women as have able bodies to work, and such children of about twelve years, whose husbands or parents are dead or gone beyond the seas, or friends to maintain them, or means of their own to preserve them from starving, may be taken up by the overseer of the poor, and that to prevent the said persons from starving, the overseers are hereby authorised to treat with merchants for the transplanting the said persons into some English plantation in America.

Commissioners [of Parliament] for Ordering and
Settling the Affairs of Ireland, July 1653

Administration

Cromwell became Lord Protector of England in 1653. The office of Lord Deputy of Ireland was revived in 1654, and a Council of State was established. The Irish parliament was dissolved, but thirty Irish members could sit in the English parliament instead (a separate Irish parliament was re-established after the eventual restoration of Charles II). Charles Fleetwood became Lord Deputy of Ireland. The Council of State followed the policy of transplantation with severity, and parliament in London began to be worried by its brutality. Maximum economic and personal destruction was being caused, with very negative effects in both countries. In 1657 Henry Cromwell, son of Oliver, replaced Fleetwood as Lord Deputy. The policy of wholesale transplantation ended, and the persecution of Catholic priests relaxed slightly.

> *Forasmuch as the within Mrs Mary Wolverston [of Stillorgan, Dublin], by reason of the bad weather that hath happened, was disabled to travel with her provision and carriages into Connaught by the tyme limited in the within passe, these are therefore to desire all whom it may concern to permit the said Mary, and the within named persons her servants, with such corne and other necessary provisions as she or they shall have with them, quietly to pass into Connaught aforesaid to their habitations, she and they behaving themselves as becometh.*
>
> *Thomas Herbert, Clerk of the Council.*
> *Dated the 14th October, 1654.*

The abiding image of the Cromwellian settlement: nineteenth-century woodcut showing troopers seizing Irish children for the slave gangs of Barbados

Upon reading the petition of the Lord of Ikerrin, and consideration hath thereof, and the report of the Standing Committee of Officers thereupon; It is thought fit and ordered, that the petitioner (in regard of his weakness and infirmity of body) be permitted to repair to the Bath in England (according to his physician's advice), in order to the recovery of his health, for the space of six weeks. And it is further ordered, that the said Lord of Ikerrin's lady be dispensed with from her transplantation into Connaught for the space of two months from the 1st day of May next; and that her servants be also dispensed with from their transplantation until they have gathered in their next harvest.

Dublin, the 24th of April, 1654
Charles Fleetwood, Miles Corbett, John Jones

Connollagh Barony

We, the said Commissioners, do hereby certify, that John Fitzgerald of Finntanstown, in the county and barony aforesaid, hath upon the 10th day of January, 1653, in pursuance of a Declaration of the Commissioners of the Parliament of the Commonwealth of England for the Affairs of Ireland, bearing date the 14th day of October, 1652, delivered unto us in writing the names of himself, and of such other persons as are to remove with him, with the quantities and qualities of their stocks and tillage, the contents whereof are as followeth: viz. The said John Fitzgerald, aged thirtie-five years; middle stature; black hair. Sarah, his wife, aged twenty-six years; brown hair; tall stature. David Fitzgerald, aged four years; black hair. His two daughters, called Joan and Mary, under the age of two years, flaxen hair. Edmund Fitzgerald, tenant, aged thirty years; tall stature; flaxen hair. Ellen, his wife, aged forty years; tall stature; brown hair. Elleanor, Margaret, and Eliza, three daughters of the said Edmund, all under the age of four years. David Wolfe, gentleman, aged twenty-four years; black hair; middle stature. Mauria Manning, aged twenty-six years; middle stature; black hair. Dermod Halpin, aged twenty-four years; tall stature; flaxen hair. Donough McCarty, aged thirty-six years; middle stature; black hair. Ann ny McNamara, servant, aged forty years; black hair; tall stature. His substance — twenty-four garrans, three cows, two sows; four acres of winter corn. The substance whereof we believe to be true. In witness whereof we have hereunto set our hands and seals, the 10th day of January, 1653.

People tried to delay being transplanted, but the authorities became impatient, and began courts martial in March 1655 to force families to move. Counties which had originally been allocated to Irish Catholics, such as Sligo and Leitrim, were clawed back to meet the urgent needs of the soldiers, and the Irish Catholics who had moved to them had to transplant yet again. Because of the lack of surveys, many people arrived in the west to find complete confusion as to where they were to go, and local commissioners often took the opportunity to accept bribes, or to seize land for themselves.

> *Sir Nicholas Comyn, numb at one side of his body of a dead palsy, accompanied only by his lady, Catherine Comyn, aged thirty-five years, middle stature; and one maidservant, Honor ny McNamara, aged twenty years, brown hair, middle stature; having no substance, but expecting the benefit of his qualification....*
>
> *Pierce, Viscount Ikerrin, going with seventeen persons, four cows, five garrans, twenty-four sheep and two swine, and claiming against sixteen acres of winter corn....*

> *Ignatius Stacpole of Limerick, orphant, aged eleven years, flaxen haire, full face, low stature; Katherine Stacpoole, orphant, sister to the said Ignatius, aged eight years, flaxen haire, full face; having no substance to relieve themselves, but desireth the benefit of his claim before the commissioners of the revenue.*

By the end of 1656 it had to be admitted that many of those who had lost their land without compensation, because of their perceived guilt, had nevertheless managed to acquire land in Connaught. Many more who were rightfully entitled to land had failed to get any at all. It is probable that bribery was rampant, and personal contacts were used to gain any advantage. A Sir Richard Barnewall, for example, had access to Oliver Cromwell himself, and ended up with a large grant of land despite his earlier political activities.

Citty of Limerick

We, the said Commissioners, doe herely certify that Margaret Heally, alias Creagh, the relict of John Heally, Esq., dead, of the county of Limerick, hath upon the 19th day of December, 1653 ... delivered unto us in writing the names of herself and of such othere persons as are to remove with her ... viz. — The said Margaret, adged thirty years; flaxen hair; full face, middle size. In substance, two cows, three ploughs of garrans, and two acres of barley and whete sowen. John Neal, her servant, adged twenty-eight years; red haire; middle stature; full face. Gennet Comyn, one of her servants, adged twenty-four years; brown haire; slender face; of middle stature. Joan Keane, servant adged thirtie-six years; brown haire; middle size; full face; and her little daughter, adged six yeares. Out of the above substance she payeth contribution....

Book of Transplanters' Certificates

In June 1657, an 'act for the attainder of the rebels in Ireland' essentially declared that the transplantation was over, and that all who had been transplanted could be considered as being pardoned for any treason they had committed. However, no further claim for a pardon could be made after 1 June 1658. Those refusing to transplant were still being punished for not moving, though it seemed hard to blame them when they knew there was no land for them to go to. By the time of the restoration of Charles II in 1660, the Cromwellian Settlement was still incomplete, and many native Irish were left where they were, by default.

The largest transformation caused by the Cromwellian Settlement was that of the landed class. Protestantism was now the proof of reliability, and a Protestant Ascendancy began to emerge; there were almost no Catholic landowners any longer. Henry Cromwell encouraged the coming together of the Protestant Anglo-Irish and the new settlers, in the interests of Protestantism. There was a change of heart about Catholics, too; instead of being pressured to convert, they were simply set aside and ignored. Priests were transported if caught, and had to live among the bogs and mountains. The Irish tradition of the

'Mass-rock' (an isolated outdoor site where Mass was said) dates from this period. Efforts were made to clear Catholics out of towns completely, but by 1659 they made up 60–80 per cent of the urban population, apart from Dublin, where they were only 26 per cent.

We have three beasts to destroy that lay heavy burdens on us. The first is the wolf, on whom we lay five pounds a head if a dog, and ten pounds if a bitch. The second beast is a priest, on whose head we lay ten pounds — if he be eminent, more. The third beast is a Tory [Irish outlaw] on whose head, if he be a public Tory, we lay twenty pounds and forty shillings on a private Tory. Your army cannot catch them. The Irish bring them in: brothers and cousins cut one another's throats.

Major Anthony Morgan, MP for Wicklow,
addressing parliament, June 1657

I judge it to be displeasing to God to join in near relations with the people of such abominations, persons whose principles have led them to the shedding of so much innocent blood as they have done ... a great hazard to the cause and work we are engaged in. I therefore think fit to let all know, that if any Officer or Souldier of this army, shall marry with any of the Women of this Nation that are Papists, or have lately been such, and whose change of Religion, is not or cannot be judged (by fit persons such as shall be appointed for that end) to flow from a reall work of God upon their hearts ... shall thereby be judged, and held uncapable of command, or trust in this Army.... And I desire all Officers of this Army, and others under my Command, that they doe their utmost (in the use of all lawful meanes) to prevent any such sinfull contracts, the issue of which can be no other than to provoke God to depart from us, or testifie his displeasure against us some way or other.

Proclamation by General Ireton, 1 May 1651

Extract from a rare copy of a Cromwellian debenture, by which former soldiers were settled in Ireland (Collection of J.P. Prendergast)

LETTER TO HON ROBERT MOLESWORTH, 'TRUE WAY TO RENDER IRELAND HAPPY AND SECURE;
OR A DISCOURSE WHEREIN 'TIS SHOWN THAT 'TIS THE INTEREST BOTH OF ENGLAND AND
IRELAND TO ENCOURAGE FOREIGN PROTESTANTS TO PLANT IN IRELAND', 1697

We cannot so much wonder at this [degeneration] when we consider how many there
are of the children of Oliver's soldiers in Ireland who cannot speak one word of
English.... This misfortune is owing to the marrying Irishwomen for want of
English, who come not over in so great numbers as are requisite. Tis sure that no
Englishman in Ireland knows what his children may be as things are now; they can-
not well live in the country without growing Irish; for none take such care as Sir
Jerome Alexander, who left his estate to his daughter, but made the gift void if she
married any Irishman....

A fateful wound hath made of me a hulk of sadness,
Stretched in fitful weakness, robbed of active vigour,
Since the martial genius of those sturdy soldiers
To earth is stricken and their valour's record silenced.

To take their place there will come the fat rumped jeerers,
After crushing them, their culture, and their cities,
Laden all with packs of plates and brass and pewter,
With shaven jaws and English and braggart accent.

Every dowdy then will wear a cape of beaver
And don a gown of silk from poll of head to ankle
All our castles will be held by clownish upstarts
Crowded full with veterans of cheese and pottage.

Dáibhí Ó Bruadair, Co. Cork poet, 1652
(translated from the Irish)

Catholic Martyrs before General Ireton, left by Cromwell to pacify the country

5: Lord Protector

L eaving Ireland in May 1650, Cromwell's next task was to confront the Scots, with whom the Prince of Wales had taken refuge. Scottish leaders had been shocked at the execution of Charles I, as monarchy was not abolished in Scotland as it had been in England, Ireland and Wales. At the Battle of Dunbar, on 3 September, which Cromwell always considered a for tunate date for him, 3,000 Scots were killed and 10,000 prisoners taken. The Scots cause had been rejected by the Lord, and 'my weak faith had been upheld,' Cromwell said. He was described afterwards by a colleague as being filled with a 'divine impulse': 'He did laugh so excessively as if he had been drunk, and his eyes sparkled with spirits.'

He again became ill after this battle, and from now on his health was in decline. He was 52 years old, and in his time would have been considered an old man. War with Scotland continued, and on 6 August 1651, Charles II was proclaimed King in Perth. However, English royalists disliked the Scots, and seemed to be reluctant to go to war side by side with them. Exactly one year after Dunbar, on 3 September 1651, Cromwell's forces inflicted a crushing defeat on the Scots at Worcester. This was the last battle Cromwell ever fought in person. The Scottish parliament was abolished, and an English army was stationed in Scotland. A Scottish preacher blasted Cromwell as being worse than the devil, 'for the scripture said, Resist the Devil and he will flie from you – but resist Oliver and he will flie in your face'.

> *By your hard and subtle words you have begotten prejudice in those who do too much (in matters of conscience, wherein every soul is to answer for itself to God) depend upon you.... Your own guilt is too much for you to bear; bring not therefore upon yourselves the blood of innocent men, deceived with pretences of King and Covenant, from whose eyes you hide a better knowledge.... Is it therefore infallibly agreeable to the Word of God all that you say? I beseech you in the bowels of Christ think it possible that you may be mistaken.... There may be a Covenant made with death and hell.*
>
> *Cromwell's manifesto to ministers of Kirk,*
> *August 1650, before the Battle of Dunbar*

England was still ruled by the 'Rump Parliament'. It was debating whether to dissolve itself and hold elections under a new, wider franchise, or return to the idea of a monarchy, but it suddenly decided instead to introduce a bill to prolong its own life. Cromwell, ever the man of action, burst violently into the House of Commons with his supporters, proclaiming that the members had 'sat long enough'. Parliament was cleared by his soldiers at the point of the sword. He said later, 'I did not think to have done this, but perceiving the spirit of God so strong upon me, I would not consult with flesh and blood at all.' The basis of his power was always his army, but they were now becoming restless at the slow progress to a wider democracy, and their pay was in arrears again.

A Decemvirate (group of ten) was set up to govern, with Cromwell at the head and Colonel John Lambert as first president. Rumours spread that Cromwell was seeking a crown for

St Giles' Cathedral in Scotland, an important centre for the Church of Scotland at the time of Cromwell

himself. He was not a republican by conviction; but he was a pragmatic politician and would do what seemed to him to be best for the country. He stated, 'If there be any that makes many poor to make a few rich, that suits not a commonwealth.'

England was a commercial rival to the Protestant Netherlands, who had also thrown off monarchy. The Netherlands were trading with English colonies abroad, and the Commonwealth declared that it had a right to search the Dutch ships, to prevent treasonous messages from being passed. War was declared in summer of 1652, and the Dutch admiral, Tromp, defeated the English navy in November. However, the English Admiral Blake defeated the Dutch navy in early 1654. In 1653, the army's pay was cut in order to pay the sailors, and to help in the building of thirty new frigates. The war was costing £1 million per year, and lasted until May 1654.

Cromwell summoned a new parliament for July 1653, known as the 'Barebones Parliament' because of the name of one member, Praise-God Barebones. This broke up in disorder in December over the question of abolition of tithes (payment for church ministers), which was interpreted by opponents as an attack on landlords and property rights. Again, members had to be forcibly cleared from the chamber. Meanwhile, another royalist rising, in which some army Levellers had joined, was defeated.

Lambert produced a document called the *Instrument for Government*, outlining a method for governing the country. This provided for an elected Protector who would have legislative authority, but who would share executive authority with a

Council of State whenever parliament was not sitting. There was one obvious choice for the job, and at the age of 54, Oliver Cromwell became Lord Protector of England.

Cromwell, our chief of men, who through a cloud
Not of warr only, but detractions rude,
Guided by faith and matchless fortitude,
To peace and truth thy glorious way hast ploughed,
And on the neck of crowned fortune proud
Hast rear'd God's trophies, and his work pursued,
While Darwen stream with blood of Scots imbrued,
And Dunbarr field resounds thy praises loud,
And Worcester's laureat wreath. Yet much remaines
To conquer still....

John Milton, 1652

Cromwell as Lord Protector

Cromwell and his family moved into the palace at Whitehall in April 1654, and also took over Hampton Court Palace. He was attacked for taking on royal powers and trappings because he was addressed as 'Your Highness', and his Council of State was referred to as the Privy Council. He seems to have led a fairly quiet life in these opulent surroundings. Piety was still the mainstay of his character, but he took pleasure in music and, particularly, the company of his family. During his Protectorship, his two youngest daughters married and the celebrations were magnificent, lasting for several days.

He had a riding accident in September, which left him lame for a while, and in November his mother died – a great grief. Her last words to him were, 'The Lord cause His face to shine upon you, and comfort you in all your adversities, and enable you to do great things for the glory of the Most High God, and to be a relief unto His People. My dear son, I leave my heart with thee.'

*Cromwell's wife receives news of his victory at Dunbar from her husband, 1650
(Drawing by Charles Seldon)*

The Death of Cromwell (Courtesy of the Victoria and Albert Museum)

*Richard Cromwell
(Courtesy of the National
Gallery of Ireland)*

*Charles II
(from the comtemporary
painting by John Greenhill)*

Parliament did not meet again until September 1654. In the meantime, Cromwell and his Council of State had produced a vast range of legislation, particularly in the area of law reform. The Spanish ambassador wrote in 1656, 'They [Cromwell and his Council] are indeed so fully occupied that they do not know which way to turn, and the Protector has not a moment to call his own'.

In September, Cromwell made his first speech before parliament as Lord Protector. It began on a peaceful note, but turned into a long harangue about the shortcomings of previous parliaments, and his hopes for improvement. This new parliament had a much larger republican element than before, and long debates took place on the nature of government. Parliament wanted to reduce the size of the army, and its costs, and insisted on having the final say on this, but Cromwell would not agree. He dismissed the members in January 1655, saying 'Instead of peace and settlement, instead of mercy and truth being brought together ... weeds and nettles, briars and thorns have thriven under your shadow.'

A badly-planned expedition was sent to seize the West Indies from Spain, but the English troops were defeated at Hispaniola, in April 1655. This was the first military defeat in the field that the Commonwealth had suffered under Cromwell, and it was a severe psychological blow. A colony was set up in Jamaica, but did not prosper for a long time. However, in international affairs Cromwell was now a notable figure. He joined with France to fight the Spanish Netherlands after Charles II turned for support to Spain, and English ships captured the Spanish treasure-fleet in September 1656. England was regaining the influence in Europe which it had lost after Charles I's overthrow. Coins were produced showing Cromwell in profile, crowned with a laurel wreath.

An experimental plan for regional government, under the control of Major-Generals, ended in failure. The Major-Generals were to have not only a military role, raising and financing local militias, but also a high level of civil authority, controlling social gatherings and sporting occasions. Many of the Major-Generals were unsuited to be governors, and acted very repressively, so the

Boscobel House in Shropshire, where Charles II sought refuge, later hiding in an oak nearby (Pitti Gallery, Florence)

abolition of the system was greeted with joy. Meanwhile, a Committee of Triers and Ejectors was examining the country's established clergy for heresy or treason, adding to an atmosphere of creeping repression and censorship.

Cromwell was becoming worn down by the cares of government, and his health continued to decline. A Leveller plot to assassinate him was foiled. He had always opposed the hereditary principle, but was having second thoughts as he could see age overcoming him. However, his son Oliver had died of smallpox in 1644, and his elder surviving son, Richard, was unsatisfactory – inclined to run up debts, he had separated from his wife. Henry Cromwell, on the other hand, his younger son, was doing well in Ireland, first as commander-in-chief and later as Lord Deputy.

In September 1656, the Second Protectoral Parliament opened; Cromwell made a speech appealing for England to be returned to a Godly state. The new Spanish War was soaking up huge sums of money, and the military still had more influence than many people thought healthy. More members of parliament, dissatisfied with the Protectorship, were coming round to the idea of restoring a king, but under much tighter control than before. In February 1657, a *Humble Petition and Advice* called for monarchy and a restored House of Lords. Cromwell was actually in favour of a second chamber, in order to exercise a balance with the House of Commons. A parliamentary bill in March established a second chamber with seventy members, all to be nominated by the Lord Protector. Under the *Humble Petition*, the powers of the Council were reduced, in favour of more powers for parliament. Meanwhile, an Anglo-French treaty against Spain was agreed, and Dunkirk came under English rule.

Moves were being made to encourage Cromwell to take on the mantle of kingship, and he seems to have been genuinely undecided about this for a long time. He objected to the actual title but John Thurloe, writing to Henry Cromwell, advised, 'The title is not the question, but it is the office, which is known to the law and this people. They know their duty to a king and his to them.' Royal status would help to give Cromwell's family and servants immunity from royalist revenge after his death; it might also protect his life, as the murder of a king was still treason. He had to be convinced that the Godly wanted this; he did not want to be accused of being self-seeking. 'I would not build Jericho again,' he said.

But his beloved army was adamantly opposed to the idea. In the end, when some of his most trusted advisers expressed their absolute abhorrence of a return to monarchy, he seemed genuinely relieved to turn down the offer. However, an elaborate investiture ceremony was held for the Lord Protector in June 1657 which sounds to all intents and purposes like a coronation. It could be argued that by rejecting the crown, he was retaining more actual authority for himself, because a king would inevitably be bound by constitutional restrictions, and the Protector was not.

Cromwell opened the new parliament in January 1658; he was depressed and ill. The large republican element in the house began to argue against the establishment of the new second chamber. There may also have been protests at what was seen to be rapidly becoming a dictatorship. He made a violent speech attacking the parliament ('Let God judge between you and me') and dissolved it in February, leaving himself and his Council in control.

His health continued to go downhill rapidly, not helped by the long and painful death of his favourite daughter, Elizabeth (or Bettie), on 6 August. He never recovered from this blow, and began to suffer fits and a recurrence of his malarial infection. He may also have suffered from blood-poisoning. He died on his 'fortunate date', 3 September, aged 59, comforted that he was dying in the grace of God. The Lord Protector had been empowered to choose his own successor, and at the last minute, he seems to have indicated his son Richard for the post.

His funeral was celebrated on 23 November with immense pomp, at a cost of £28,000. There were complaints at this waste, to which it was said he would undoubtedly have objected: '...I was persuaded if it had been asked him in his lifetime if such work should be acted about him ... I believe he would have denied it and said it shall not be thus with me when I am dead,' wrote Edward Burroughs. His body had actually been buried in Westminster Abbey shortly after death, possibly because the embalming process had gone wrong, and it was an empty coffin that took centre stage at the funeral. A wax figure had been used for the lying-in-state, copying what had been done at James I's funeral. Surprisingly, there was no funeral oration dwelling on the deceased's piety and virtues – normally an important part of a Puritan funeral.

Cromwell had not been particularly loved by the people, and there were very few signs of popular mourning. He had been blamed for the excesses of the Major-Generals, the level of taxation, the oppressive Puritanism of society. John Evelyn's diary entry reads: '...the joyfullest funeral that I ever saw; for there was none cried but dogs, which the soldiers hooted away with a barbarous noise, drinking and taking tobacco in the streets as they went.' However, his old colleague John Thurloe, secretary of the

Cromwell was not by nature a democrat; here he storms out of Parliament before acting against it.

Council of State, confessed, 'I am not able to speak or write, this stroke is so sore.... I can do nothing but put my mouth in the dust and say It is the Lord.'

Aftermath

Richard Cromwell took over as Lord Protector, but was not capable of retaining his father's firm command of the parliament. Moreover, he had to be granted immunity from arrest for his huge personal debts. The country was suffering an economic recession, and riots broke out. Charles Fleetwood joined an anti-Richard party, led by the army, which called for the return of the old 'Long Parliament'. Richard resigned in May, Lambert led a military coup, and a semi-military junta began to rule, only to collapse in December 1659. In the end, General Monck took control, and urged Charles II to return to his kingdom. The Long Parliament dissolved itself in March, and the restored king arrived in triumph in May 1660 – the man of whom Cromwell had said, 'Give him a shoulder of mutton and a whore, that's all he cares for'. Richard Cromwell ('Tumbledown Dick') managed to get himself to the continent, and lived in retirement until 1712.

The Cromwell family as a whole was left in peace after the restoration. The Lady Protectress, Elizabeth, died peacefully in 1665. Henry Cromwell was allowed to keep his Irish lands, and retired to Cambridgeshire. However, peace was not to be his father's lot, even after death. The bodies of Oliver Cromwell, his son-in-law Henry Ireton, and John Bradshaw (president of the commission at Charles I's trial) were exhumed in January 1661, dragged through the streets of London on hurdles, hanged on the Tyburn gallows and finally decapitated. The heads were placed on pikes at Westminster Hall, and remained there until 1684. Oliver's head now rests in Sidney Sussex College, Cambridge, although the exact burial-spot is kept a close secret.

George Monck, later Duke of Abermarle, soldier turned conciliator, who brought about the restoration

Epilogue

English Legacy

Even in his own lifetime, Oliver Cromwell was a man very difficult to comprehend, whose character was interpreted in a dozen different ways – pious or hypocritical, blood-thirsty or compassionate, self-controlled or frenzied – and he could be all of these.

In matters of religion, he was a stern individualist. Rejecting organised religion, he wrestled with God by himself, seeking to find the way of the Lord. He needed to be convinced that his path was right, and he saw success as a sign that the Lord was with him. He recognised the right of every individual to take this path, and it annoyed him that some men tried to force others to worship in one way only: 'Nothing will satisfy them unless they can put their finger upon their brethren's consciences, to pinch them there.' However, religious freedom had its limitations for him. He was tolerant of Presbyterians, Independents and Baptists, but not of Quakers, Anglicans or Roman Catholics. It is sometimes given as an example of his tolerance that he wanted to have the Jews readmitted to England (they had been officially expelled in the thirteenth century), but this may have been linked to a belief that the Millennium could not arrive until all Jews were converted to Christianity. Obviously, they could not be converted while they were out of reach.

Three lives of Cromwell were published after his death, and before the restoration of Charles II. One, by an anonymous 'L.S.', gives the following picture:

> His speeches were for the most part ambiguous, especially in public meetings, wherein he left others to pick out the meaning than did it himself. But when offenders came under his own examination, then would he speak plain English and declare his power unto them in a ranting style.... The pride and ambition which some say he was guilty of, may be easily excused as an original sin inherent in nature.... In [his #religion] he was zealous, not altogether like the Pharisee that prayed in the Temple; but really often would he mourn in secret and many times his eyes in public distil tears at the Nation's stubbornness.

Even Edward Hyde, a royalist whose daughter later married James II, said of Cromwell, 'He could never have done half that mischief without great parts of industry and judgment.'

Edward Burroughs, although he wrote that Oliver Cromwell would have disapproved of the extravagant show of his funeral, continued: '...though he was once zealous against popery, yet he did too much forget the good cause, and too much sought the greatness and honour of the world and loved the praise of men and took flattering titles and vain respects of deceitful men.' Richard Baxter, a pastor, said much the same: '[Cromwell] meant honestly in the main, and was pious and conscionable in the main course of his life, till Prosperity and Success corrupted him.'

He was often accused of hypocrisy. Lilburne the Leveller said of him, 'You shall scarce speak to Cromwell about anything, but he will lay his hand on his breast, elevate his eyes and call God to record. He will weep, howl and repent, even while he doth smite you under the fifth rib.' Many of his old colleagues felt betrayed, as he left them behind and moved on. He was driven by one thing only — loyalty to God — not to men or to men's works. His soldiers followed him gladly, as a strong commander, although, as one said, 'I'll tell you a common proverb that we had among us of the General, that in the field he was the graciousest and most gallant man in the world, but out of the field, and when he came home again to government, the worst.'

It was inevitable that after the restoration a large number of histories were published, damning Oliver Cromwell and the Commonwealth, and accusing them all of unspeakable crimes, beginning with the regicide. His legacy is incredibly mixed, and his name still provokes an emotional response, either of loathing or of deep respect. Even in England, where he is by and large well regarded, a borough in Oxfordshire refused to name a housing estate after him in the mid-twentieth century. During the First World War, Winston Churchill, for whom Cromwell was a hero, wanted to name a battleship for him, but this was vetoed by King George V because he was a regicide. He was always popular with fighting men, but the erection of his statue outside Westminster Abbey was a source of controversy.

As a matter of fact, the end of his rule and the Commonwealth began to be regretted during the ramshackle, high-spending, dissolute reign of Charles II, when the court seemed to be leaning towards popery again, and the king sank deeper and deeper into debt with France. In his famous diaries, Samuel Pepys wrote of a friend: '[he] doth say that the court is in a way to ruin all for their pleasures; and says that he himself hath once taken the liberty to tell the King the necessity of having at least a show of religion in the government, and sobriety; and that it was that that did set up and keep up Oliver, though he was the greatest rogue in the world.... Why will not people lend their money? Why will they not trust the King as well as Oliver?' The poet Andrew Marvell, who flourished during both the Commonwealth and the Restoration, later wrote:

> De Witt and Cromwell had each a brave soul
> I freely declare it, I am for Old Noll
> Though his government did a tyrant resemble
> He made England great and his enemies tremble.

Irish Legacy

In Ireland, we all know what to believe of Cromwell and his bloodthirsty crew; we were taught it at school. When it comes to battle statistics, Drogheda and Wexford seem small beer after the carnage of the English Civil Wars, or the Irish Nine Years' War, or any number of battles in previous centuries. Surely other military leaders had done equivalent damage, yet their names are now forgotten, and Cromwell's is a byword. It seems probable, however, that the massacres in these two towns, however inconclusive the actual numbers of dead, were peculiarly horrible in their coldblooded ruthlessness. The memories they left behind were too strong to be erased. They may have grown in exaggerated tales as years went by, but the original events left an indelible mark. It was not a matter of imagination. The Settlement which changed the face of Ireland bore his name also, and gave plenty of ammunition for the 'Curse of Cromwell'.

Another Cromwellian legacy is the postal system, which was established in 1657. This was not just for the good of the people, of course; it abolished all private postal systems and established a government monopoly, so the profits went to the state. It also gave the state the right to intercept letters and open them, so as 'to discover and prevent many dangerous and wicked Designs, which have been, and are daily contrived against the Peace and Welfare of this Commonwealth'.

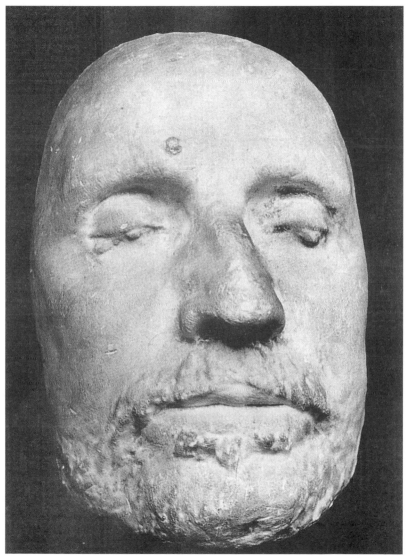

The death mask of Oliver Cromwell

Bibliography

Adamson, John, 'Strafford's Ghost: The British Context of Viscount Lisle's Lieutenancy of Ireland', in Ohlmeyer, *Ireland from Independence to Occupation*

Barber, Sarah, 'Scotland and Ireland under the Commonwealth: a question of loyalty', in Ellis, S. and Barber, S. (eds.), *Conquest and Union: Fashioning a British State 1485–1725*, London 1995

Barnard, T.C., *Cromwellian Ireland: English Government and Reform in Ireland 1649–60*, Oxford 1975

— 'Settling and Unsettling Ireland – The Cromwellian and Williamite revolutions', in Ohlmeyer, *Ireland from Independence to Occupation*

— 'The Protestant Interest 1641–1660', in Ohlmeyer, *Ireland from Independence to Occupation*

Bartlett, T. and Jeffrey, K. (eds.), *A Military History of Ireland*, Cambridge 1996

Berresford Ellis, Peter, *Hell or Connaught! The Cromwellian Colonisation of Ireland 1652–1660*, Belfast 1980 (reprint)

Bryce, G. et al. (eds.), *Political Thought in Ireland Since the Seventeenth Century*, London 1993

Buchan, John, *Oliver Cromwell*, London 1941 (reprint)

Canny, Nicholas, *From Reformation to Restoration: Ireland 1534–1660*, Dublin 1987

— 'What Really Happened in Ireland in 1641?', in Ohlmeyer, *Ireland from Independence to Occupation*

Carlyle, T. (ed. by S.C. Lomas), *Oliver Cromwell's Letters and Speeches* (three vols.), London 1904

Clarke, Aidan, '1659 and the road to Restoration', in Ohlmeyer, *Ireland from Independence to Occupation*

Corish, P.J., *The Catholic Community in the Seventeenth and Eighteenth Centuries*, Dublin 1981

— 'Ormond, Rinuccini and the Confederates, 1645–49', in Moody, Martin & Byrne, *New History of Ireland III*

— 'The Cromwellian Conquest, 1649–53', in Moody, Martin & Byrne, *New History of Ireland III*

— 'The Cromwellian Regime, 1650–60', in Moody, Martin & Byrne, *New History of Ireland III*

— 'The Rising of 1641 and the Catholic Confederacy, 1641–45', in Moody, Martin & Byrne, *New History of Ireland III*

Coward, Barry, *Oliver Cromwell*, London 1991

Firth, C.H., *Cromwell's Army*, London 1902 (reprint 1992)

Fitzpatrick, Brendan, S*eventeenth Century Ireland: The War of Religions*, Dublin 1988

Fraser, Antonia, *Cromwell, Our Chief of Men*, London 1973 (republished 1999)

Gaunt, Peter, *The British Wars 1637–51*, London 1997

Gentles, Ian, *The New Model Army in England, Ireland and Scotland 1645–1653*, London 1991

Gillespie, Raymond, 'The Irish Economy at War 1641–52', in Ohlmeyer, *Ireland from Independence to Occupation*

Gillingham, John, *Cromwell, Portrait of a Soldier*, London 1976

Hill, Christopher, *God's Englishman: Oliver Cromwell and the English Revolution*, London 1970

Kilroy, P., 'Radical Religion in Ireland 1641–1660', in Ohlmeyer, *Ireland from Independence to Occupation*

Lindley, Keith, *The English Civil War and Revolution, A Sourcebook*, London 1998

Loeber, R. and Parker, G., 'The Military Revolution in seventeenth-century Ireland', in Ohlmeyer, *Ireland from Independence to Occupation*

McKenny, Kevin, 'The seventeenth-century land settlement in Ireland: towards a statistical interpretation', in Ohlmeyer, *Ireland from Independence to Occupation*

Moody, T.W., Martin, F.X. and Byrne, F.J. (eds.), *A New History of Ireland Volume III: Early Modern Ireland 1534–1691*, Oxford 1976

Morrill, John (ed.), *Oliver Cromwell and the English Revolution*, London 1990

Ohlmeyer, Jane, 'Ireland independent: Confederate foreign policy and international relations during the mid-seventeenth century', in Ohlmeyer, *Ireland from Independence to Occupation*

— (ed.), *Ireland from Independence to Occupation 1641–60*, Cambridge 1995

Paul, R.S., *The Lord Protector: Religion and Politics in the Life of Oliver Cromwell*, 1955

Perceval-Maxwell, M., *The Outbreak of the Irish Rebellion of 1641*, Dublin 1994

Prendergast, J.P., *The Cromwellian Settlement of Ireland*, London 1865 (reprint 1996)

Reilly, Tom, *Cromwell, An Honourable Enemy*, Dingle 1999

Roots, I., *Cromwell: A Profile*, London 1973

Sherwood, Roy, *King in All But Name*, London 1997

Shiels, W. (ed.), *Persecution and Toleration: Studies in Church History*, 1984

Wheeler, James Scott, *Cromwell in Ireland*, Dublin 1999

Wheeler, James Scott, 'Four Armies in Ireland', in Ohlmeyer, *Ireland from Independence to Occupation*

Young, Peter, *Naseby 1645: The Campaign and the Battle*, London 1985

Index

Also in this series

The Irish Famine
An Illustrated History
by Helen Litton
ISBN 0-86327-427-7
£6.99

Irish Rebellions 1798–1916
An Illustrated History
by Helen Litton
ISBN 0-86327-634-2
£6.99

The Celts
An Illustrated History
by Helen Litton
ISBN 0-86327-577-X
£6.99

The Irish Civil War
An Illustrated History
by Helen Litton
ISBN 0-86327-480-3
£6.99

Available from:

Wolfhound Press
68 Mountjoy Square
Dublin 1
Tel: (353-1) 874 0354
Fax: (353-1) 8720207

THE

IRISH FAMINE

AN ILLUSTRATED HISTORY

The Irish Famine is an account of one of the most significant — and tragic — events in Irish history. Helen Litton deals with the emotive subject of the Great Famine clearly and succinctly, documenting the causes and their effects.

With quotes from first-hand accounts, and relying on the most up-to-date studies, the author describes the mixture of ignorance, confusion, inexperience and vested interests that lay behind the 'good *v* evil' image of popular perception.

A story of individuals and of a society in crisis, it should be read by anyone who seeks a fuller understanding of the Irish past.

IRISH REBELLIONS

1798–1916
AN ILLUSTRATED HISTORY

'a useful little volume ... which summarises the various conflicts
and gives an idea of the social context.
The illustrations are wonderful.'
Sunday Tribune

From the time that Britain first began to take
interest in the country on her western side,
the history of the two islands has been one
of constant struggle. Each generation of Irish
rebels left a speech, a watchword or a martyr,
which could be passed on to encourage
passion and idealism. Once Britain had been
driven out, prosperity and universal harmony
would follow. This was the dream.

Using newspaper reports, speeches, eye-
witness accounts and a mass of photographs
and illustrative material, Helen Litton turns
her accessible style to the major events of
1798, 1803, 1848, 1867 and 1916.

*Irish Rebellions 1798–1916: An Illustrated
History* is a clear and informative survey of the
most well-known rebellions of Irish history.

THE CELTS

AN ILLUSTRATED HISTORY

'A small book which manages ... to pack in
a hugh amount of information.'
Sunday Tribune

'The Celts are terrifying in appearance. They
are tall, with moist white flesh; their hair is
naturally blond ... They wear amazing clothes:
tunics dyed in every colour ... They are boast-
ers and threateners and yet they are quick of
mind. They have also lyric poets whom they
call Bards and certain philosophers whom
they call Druids.'

Diodorus Siculus (First century BC)

From Julius Caesar writing on the Celts to
reconstructed dwellings, strange bog bodies,
exotic archaeological finds, Celtic gods, the
cult of the human head and the beauty of
La Tene Celtic art, numerous illustrations,
photographs and quotations paint a capti-
vating and surprising picture of this unique
race.

In *Celts: An Illustrated History* Helen Litton
explores Celtic Europe, Britain and Ireland —
from the eighth century BC to the fifth
century AD — with a particular focus on
Ireland, the last bastion of the Celtic world.

THE IRISH

CIVIL WAR

AN ILLUSTRATED HISTORY

'The Illustrations are many and fascinating, the text ... lucid and informative in its own right.'
The Irish Times

In this concise history Helen Litton recounts the events leading up to the signing of the Treaty, the impassioned Dáil debates which followed, the destruction of the Four Courts and the confused fighting of the Civil War itself.

Here are the pragmatism of Arthur Griffith, the charisma of Michael Collins, the resounding rhetoric of de Valera, the military tactics of Liam Lynch. Here also are the women of the Cumann na mBan, and the war-weary civilians who had just begun to rebuild their lives from the ashes of the War of Independence.

The Irish Civil War: An Illustrated History will provide a stimulating re-think for all who know the period well, and an informative introduction for those who want to understand it for the first time.